Greenhouse Gardening

Greenhouse Gardening

Peter Blackburne-Maze

THE CROWOOD PRESS

First published in 2012 by
The Crowood Press Ltd
Ramsbury, Marlborough
Wiltshire SN8 2HR

www.crowood.com

© Peter Blackburne-Maze 2012

British Library Cataloguing-in-Publication Data
A catalogue record for this book is available from the British Library.

ISBN 978 1 84797 335 1

Typeset by SR Nova Pvt Ltd., Bangalore, India
Printed and bound in Singapore by Craft Print International Ltd

Contents

Introduction

Greenhouse Gardening has two main aims: to encourage anyone who already has a greenhouse to widen their interest and to inspire the purely 'outdoor' gardener to buy one.

There are three main purposes of a greenhouse: first, to enable a gardener, existing or potential, to grow plants that would not thrive, or even survive, outdoors in Britain. Such plants range from the exotics that come from the warmer parts of the world to those that will survive outdoors but will fail to thrive. Second, a greenhouse can enable a gardener to produce plants out of their natural season. These fall into two groups: half-hardies and wholly tender plants. Half-hardies need to be started under protection early in the year and are then planted outside to mature and complete their life. The group includes such plants as French marigolds and ridge cucumbers. The wholly tender plants, which can be both useful and ornamental, need the lifelong protection of a greenhouse to survive and include, for example, indoor plants such as the Rubber plant (*Ficus elastica*) and indoor varieties of tomato.

Even an unheated greenhouse will allow the gardener to grow plants successfully that he or she would otherwise either not be able to grow at all, or be able to grow only unsatisfactorily.

Before making the decision to buy a greenhouse, there must be some forward planning. First, is there a suitable place for it in the garden? It should be sheltered but not in the shade. A spot too close to trees is not only likely to be too dark for good results, but could also lead to difficulties with leaves in the autumn and branches coming down in a gale. It is also a benefit to have the greenhouse reasonably near the house, although not essential. 'Out of sight' can also be 'out of mind', once the novelty has worn off. The ground should be level, or nearly level, and mains water nearby is very useful.

With so many aids to greenhouse gardening relying on electricity, access to a power source is more or less a 'must' today if all the potential benefits are to be enjoyed. It will be needed for some types of heating, for lighting, if that is thought necessary, and for many more 'advanced' gadgets, such as propagators and most automatic watering devices. Heating a greenhouse can take growing a stage further, with an immeasurably extended range of ornamental and consumable plants.

In the spring, a greenhouse is invaluable for propagating half-hardy bedding plants and vegetables that are going to be planted and grown on outdoors. In winter, it can be used as a warm place to sit, on a sunny afternoon, if it is not full of plants.

The many benefits to owning a greenhouse must be weighed up against the initial cost and the ongoing running costs. Of course, some greenhouses are more expensive than others; similarly, some are cheaper to run than others. Probably the greatest variation in price relates to the size of the greenhouse, and to the material from which it is made – usually wood or aluminium. Aluminium is less bother to maintain and the light admission is slightly better than with wood, because the framework members are thinner for the same strength. However, wood offers greater versatility and feels more 'homely'.

A greenhouse should be a fun hobby, never a chore. It can be as much of a commitment as a pet, if it is allowed to get out of hand, so do remember always simply to enjoy it!

1   The Greenhouse

WHY HAVE A GREENHOUSE?

There are a number of reasons why people buy a greenhouse: they may have seen some magnificent half-hardy or tender plants that they would love to have, but which need to be grown in a greenhouse; they may plan to use it as a sun-house in the winter; or it may be simply that the neighbours have one! However, most people probably buy one after practising several years of outdoor gardening and then wishing to take their pastime a step further and try something new. This is undoubtedly the best way to go.

The successful greenhouse gardener is usually confident and fairly well versed in the whys and wherefores of growing plants outdoors. There is little point in spending time and money on a greenhouse without some knowledge of outdoor gardening – how do the plants work? What are their likes and dislikes? Plants under cover are far less tolerant of mistakes by their keeper than plants in the open, which have the sun and rain to help them fight against neglect. Many of the plants that the greenhouse owner chooses to attempt to grow will be total strangers, and their environment will have to be closely controlled.

The acquisition of a greenhouse should be given some serious thought. If the gardener is able to consider the world from the point of view of the plants, the process of looking after them will become quite easy, and the greenhouse will become a place of refuge and peace.

This is the sort of greenhouse, wooden and about 8ft by 6ft, that is owned by thousands of gardeners, both newcomers and the more experienced. It will fit into all but the smallest garden. It is easy to manage and the right size to start with as it is not so large as to dominate the gardener's life. Inside, it has staging on the right-hand side and room for a border on the left. Plants such as tomatoes and cucumbers can be grown or stood on one side and young or pot plants on the other. The permanent floor in the centre is of placed bricks (not cemented).

The most obvious benefit of a greenhouse is that it will greatly extend the list of plants that may be grown. Whereas outdoors is always the best permanent place for growing fully hardy plants (those that will tolerate all weathers and conditions), those that are only partially hardy, usually called half-hardies, will need at least some time under glass. They will grow reasonably happily outdoors during the frost-free period of the year but will usually be killed by the first proper frost of autumn. The half-hardies include many bedding plants, such as French and African marigolds, along with semi-hardy vegetables such as marrows, French beans and runner beans. All of these will be finished off or at least severely damaged by frost, but they can be easily raised from seed in a greenhouse and planted outside when the risk of frost is over, usually in late spring.

A number of plants are perfectly hardy outdoors for eleven months of the year, but have flowers that are ruined by frost. This small but interesting group includes pot-grown camellias. Growing these in pots is one way of enjoying them in gardens that are liable to late spring frosts – they can be allowed to flower under cover but can go outside when this is over. When they are grown outdoors, they need to be covered with fleece or similar material when they are in flower and a frost is likely.

Fully tender plants, sometimes called tropical or semi-tropical, will only tolerate being outdoors in the height of summer, if at all. These include such plants as Stephanotis, fruiting bananas and citrus trees (oranges, lemons, and so on), the best examples of which can be seen at the Palace of Versailles, outside Paris. All the trees in the world-famous Orangerie are grown in 'Versailles' tubs, kept in the Orangerie from about mid-autumn to mid-spring, and taken outside just for the summer.

Another very important reason for having a greenhouse is for raising bedding plants and half-hardy vegetables. With a bit of warmth, sowing can start in early or mid-spring and they can be ready for planting outside in their final positions in late spring. In addition, there are flowers and vegetables that can be grown in a frost-free

The Palm House at the Royal Botanic Gardens, Kew, London, has the space to house some of the largest plants that require the particular conditions that it provides. It is not so much the warmth that they need during the summer as an avoidance of the damp, cold weather that is typical of a British winter. The aerial walkway in the centre provides a fascinating bird's-eye view of the plants.

The king of orangeries is, without a doubt, and rather appropriately, the spectacular example at the Palace of Versailles outside Paris. This is a summer view with all the trees growing outdoors and in 'Versailles' tubs. It holds some 1,200 orange trees and 300 tender exotics.

environment, with the minimum of artificial heat during the winter. As well as many different salad vegetables, such as lettuces and radishes, a greenhouse can also be used for forcing other edible crops, such as seakale, chicory, strawberries and rhubarb. This business of out-of-season plants is much neglected – as well as extending the cropping season of edible crops into the autumn, a whole list of different ornamentals can be 'forced' in an unheated greenhouse.

If the greenhouse is sited in the right location – where it will catch the winter sun for the two hours or so that it shows itself above the neighbours' trees – it is easy to turn it into a conservatory during the winter with a couple of comfy chairs.

SITE CONSIDERATIONS

Once the decision has been made to buy a greenhouse, resist the temptation to go at it like a bull at a gate. It will almost certainly represent a significant capital outlay, and the wrong one may end up being an expensive disaster, so it is worth taking lots of time at this stage. First, is there enough space for it? Fortunately, greenhouses come in all shapes and sizes – even small enough to be installed on a balcony – so there will certainly be one that will fit. Any 'garden' is big enough for a greenhouse, although the chosen site will probably be the one with the least number of faults rather than the one with the most virtues.

In the past, the big house would have had equally large gardens and greenhouses to provide the household with fruit, flowers and vegetables all year round. Few still exist.

Level Ground

A sloping site is fine, as long as it is not a hill – even a north-facing slope is tolerable, although a shortage of sun might be a problem – but, clearly, the best site will be on level ground. An uneven or sloping site will need to be levelled. This is not as big a job as it might seem because it is only the footings

A fine example of a restored vinery or mixed house on a steep slope. This kind of house is often divided into sections, with a door between each. The sections can have a different temperature regime, providing for a much wider range of plants. The boiler would normally be at the lowest point, on the basis that hot water from the boiler rises and cool water sinks and returns.

of the greenhouse that need to be level; the surrounding ground can be left sloping.

When levelling, the soil should be dug out and redistributed elsewhere in the garden. The soil that has been removed from the 'uphill' end should never be used to raise the 'downhill' end. In other words, the floor of the greenhouse and the footings must be on undisturbed soil. Trying to firm built-up ground and keep the whole thing level is virtually impossible, as further settling will inevitably occur.

A sound foundation is vital for any greenhouse and, the larger the structure, the more important it is. As well as being sufficiently firm and well compacted for the footings, the site should also be largely free of organic matter. As organic matter rots and settles, so will the ground. This can cause the building to twist, which carries the risk of glass breaking under the uneven strain and of sliding doors jamming. This can be problematic if the greenhouse is going to be sited on part of a vegetable garden, and the area must be firmed down as hard as possible.

Of course, the best solution is to find a site that is already firm, such as on the edge of a lawn or on an old path or yard, although it will be harder work to dig out the footings.

Sunshine

The next important consideration is the amount of sunshine that the site gets. Clearly, a greenhouse is only going to be of benefit if it is in a sunny position, but it does not have to be in blazing sun from dawn to dusk. That is asking too much and will cause its own problems. The most important consideration is whether the site has good winter sunshine.

direction. They also have a beauty of their own.

However, these benefits are greatly reduced if the trees are tall and too close to the greenhouse or on its south side, thereby shading it from the sun during that part of the year when the sun is low or completely hidden.

Except in certain circumstances, walls are not good for sheltering greenhouses. They certainly reduce the power of the wind but at the same time they can create a turbulence that is stronger and more damaging. This was well understood in Victorian times, when wealthy estate owners would have walled gardens built. In windy locations, trees would be planted at a distance from the main house and its walled garden to reduce the power of the wind, without causing problems. On a more modern and domestic scale, it is a good idea to have shrubs and small trees in the southwest part of a garden in Britain, as this is usually the direction from which the prevailing winds come. As in the large Victorian gardens, walls and fences, both internal and on boundaries, can create turbulence rather than peace and quiet. On the other hand, a hedge in the right place simply filters the wind and slows it down. In addition, the sheltering effect from a good hedge extends as far as ten times the height of that hedge.

Where possible, any hedges near the prospective site of a greenhouse should be left. Unless they are clearly too tall and are causing excessive shading, they are probably doing an immense amount of good. It is better to plant one than take one out. Any solid object, such as a shed or house, fence or wall, is likely to cause wind turbulence, but if it has plants growing against it,

An example of the kind of greenhouse that used to be found in all large, private gardens. A vinery house was tailor-made for growing grapes. The vines were planted on the inside of the low wall and trained up the large glazed roof, giving the maximum area for cropping and perfect conditions.

Sunshine is used not only to raise the temperature in the greenhouse but also to 'supply' daylight, especially in winter. The worst combination in terms of conditions is heat and gloom, which can result in tall and thin (drawn) plants and seedlings.

It is preferable for a greenhouse to need shading in the summer than to have to light it artificially in the winter and spring. Reducing light and heat during the summer is less costly than having to increase them during the winter and spring.

Shelter

The provision of shelter from strong winds can be a two-edged sword because, even assuming that other factors are satisfactory, too much shelter can bring its own problems. The best shelter is that which is provided by trees; and it is free. Trees make the finest windbreak because they filter the wind and reduce its force rather than actually stopping it or funnelling it in another much of that harm will be turned to good by reducing the force of the wind.

Orientation

Originally, a building that was 'oriented' was pointing towards the east, or the Orient. Now, the orientation of a building is simply the direction in which a building faces in relation to the compass. In the case of a greenhouse, it is important when considering the amount of sunshine that is going to fall on it.

In the commercial glasshouse world, most growing houses with cropping plants in them run north–south. In other words, one end faces north and the other faces south. That means that the rows of plants also run north–south. With this orientation, the sun rises on the east-facing side, passes over both sides of the rows of plants and sets on the west-facing side. Thus, every plant gets the same amount of sunshine. Those on the south-facing end are slightly better off than the rest but not by enough to make a significant difference.

However, a commercial propagating house is usually orientated east–west. The plants in the house are small and will soon be moved out. Thus, with the rows and the staging running east–west, each plant receives the maximum amount of light. This can be increased by having tiered staging so that every young plant receives as much sunlight as possible.

Most domestic greenhouse gardeners do not have the luxury of choosing the direction in which their greenhouse will point and, to be honest, it is not going to make the difference between success and failure. However, if the choice is there, a north–south orientation is the best bet. This will usually give an equal amount of sun to both the staging and to the other side, where the border usually is, assuming that this is what is wanted.

If the house has to run east–west, the staging should be on the south side, so that all the young plants in seed trays and pots will be on the sunny side of the house in the spring, when the sun is at its lowest. This will give them a good start in life. The tomatoes, cucumbers, and so on, which will be producing the fresh produce, will be quite happy on the 'border' side. The plants will shortly be growing either in the border itself or in large pots or growbags, and so on, and they will soon be in the sun.

Electricity and Water

Electricity really is essential in greenhouse gardening. Without it, a greenhouse is little more than a walk-in cold frame or cloche. (The tiny ones cannot, in all honesty, be judged alongside a 'proper' greenhouse, although they are useful for accommodating a growbag with tomato plants.) Electricity powers heaters, lighting, propagators, some types of ventilator, possibly an automatic watering system; in fact, any number of desirable or essential accessories. There is no need to be either extravagant or miserly but, if you are going to have a greenhouse, it is worth doing the job properly, and making the best possible use of it.

Access to a source of electricity will therefore influence the siting of the greenhouse, as will proximity to mains water, which is also very important. It is all very well using rainwater collected from the greenhouse roof but, in a hot and/or dry summer, this may soon run out.

Greenhouse gardening on a grand scale. Greenhouses of this size were really extra rooms for the house where large, mature plants, such as palms and bananas, were often grown for their show-off value more than for their crops.

Depending on what is going to be grown in the greenhouse, it could be that proximity to the house is also important. This will be more convenient, especially if you want to grow pot plants for indoors, and will also serve to remind you not to neglect the greenhouse once its novelty has begun to wear off!

DECISIONS, DECISIONS

Cost

After all the planning and careful consideration about whether or not to go ahead, the next unavoidable step is to look at the cost involved in buying and building a greenhouse, together with all the equipment and accessories that can go with it. As with most things, buy the best you can afford, as it will last longer and give far better service than a cheaper version.

Size and Shape

When deciding on the size of the greenhouse, there are a number of issues to be considered, but it will ultimately depend on the space available and on the cost. It will also be influenced by the shape of the proposed site and on its suitability for a greenhouse. If there is plenty of space, but much of it is shaded by trees or buildings, then the choice is immediately reduced. Finally, the larger the greenhouse, the more time it will need to look after the plants that it is housing.

In the past, garden greenhouses were usually rectangular. The majority still are but, with a greater choice of materials and better engineering know-how, there are now a number of alternative shapes. From rectangular to triangular to round, a smart new greenhouse can also be a status symbol, in much the same way as a new car is. The actual shape of the greenhouse is relatively unimportant, horticulturally speaking, and the variety is largely based on personal preference.

There is one factor that is relevant when considering an unusual shape: the cost of replacement glass will be more than that of a standard rectangular piece. Young parents with children playing ball games nearby would do well to take this seriously, although glass in the greenhouse is most commonly broken by flying stones that have been launched by the blades of a rotary mower. One solution is to buy a greenhouse that uses some material other than glass for the glazing, such as acrylic. With the right choice, this virtually eliminates breakages.

A round greenhouse can either be six-sided, with standard-shaped and -sized panes of glass for the vertical sides and triangular or rhomboidal panes (four-sided with the top and bottom edges parallel but the two side edges not) for the upper ones; alternatively, the glass may be shaped and moulded to the curve of the design, to create a truly hemispherical structure. These pieces of glass are extremely expensive to replace.

The most popular (and therefore the cheapest) version is the ordinary free-standing, rectangular, 'span-roof' design. The shape is the easiest and cheapest to make; it is very versatile and is available in more or less any size. Most have the standard 24in glazing for the top and sides and already cut pieces for the ends. This is clearly the type to go for unless there are any special requirements.

Even the basic shape has its variations. The glass (or substitute material) may start at the ground – in the 'glass-to-ground' type – or it may be raised on a permanent base of 30cm (12in) or more in height. Where this base is timber, it will come as part of the greenhouse. A brick base gives the most stable structure but it will add to the cost as it will have to be built on site. The 'glass-to-ground' type is normally the one to go for, but, with either type, a base will be required on which to stand the greenhouse. This can be made of sleepers, brickwork or concrete

In the Victorian age, a large private house would frequently have an orangery, often used as a general display house. This one at Ripley Castle in Yorkshire is relatively modest in size and is about average.

beams, and some manufacturers include a concrete beam base to which the greenhouse is bolted.

There are two models that are warmer than a free-standing version. The 'lean-to' greenhouse is put against a wall (of the house or free-standing) or fence, while the 'three-quarter span' house is also a lean-to, but with the two eaves of the roof at different heights. The latter was more common in the past than it is now, and was often seen in large, Victorian walled gardens in Britain. In essence, it was a lean-to but taller than the wall. Because one side is a wall, both types offer much greater warmth than a free-standing greenhouse in the open garden, particularly when erected against a south-facing brick or stone wall.

Nowadays, such designs are usually built where circumstances prevent the use of the standard, span-roof, rectangular greenhouse. They are still available but are harder to find.

Some of the grander 'greenhouse' structures that are seen these days, often used as an extra room or a 'sun room', are not in fact greenhouses, but conservatories. The original purpose of a conservatory was as a display house for exotic plants, rather than as a 'working' greenhouse.

Material

Fifteen to twenty years ago there was a rush among manufacturers to research new glazing materials as alternatives to glass. This has been extended to alternatives for the greenhouse structure itself. It resulted in many new plastics, either used on their own or as coatings for metal, coming on to the market, with varying results. Those destined for glazing have more or less been reduced to acrylic on its own or polycarbonate coated with acrylic.

Polythene sheeting is another possible material but it is not suitable for a serious greenhouse. There are others but acrylic and/or polycarbonate are streets ahead of polythene for permanent glazing. It is also available like double-glazing units, in sheets consisting of two or even three layers; these have a much higher insulation value than a single layer. It is also, of course, much stronger. Glass is still the best material for letting the light in.

Recently, a new type of 'greenhouse' has been gaining in popularity: the polythene tunnel. This has spread into domestic gardens, large and small, from commercial nurseries. Broadly speaking, it usually consists of a series of metal hoops with polythene sheeting stretched over them. It is very much cheaper than a 'proper' greenhouse, and indeed is intended to be. It does not compare with a wood- or metal-framed structure with glass glazing, but it does serve a useful purpose when raising a significant number of plants for sale. As well as giving the plants protection, it can also be heated by an electric hot air blower. Polythene tunnels are not fully fledged greenhouses but they still have an important part to play.

At the lower end of the price scale, there are also small greenhouses with polythene glazing. These are splendid for beginners and can also be put up temporarily for jobs such as 'hardening off' (toughening) bedding plants in the spring, before they are planted outside. The life expectancy of polythene is not much over two or three years and depends on its quality and thickness. Such cheaper 'greenhouses' certainly have their place in gardens and can be useful as a less costly way of getting greenhouse experience before buying a more expensive and permanent version.

In terms of the main structure of the greenhouse, metal and wood are the two materials that are used for the vast majority of greenhouses. Even the most modern plastics and fibreglass are still either unsuitable or too expensive, or even both.

Realistically, the choice lies between aluminium and wood. Aluminium, which came on the greenhouse scene in the 1950s, is a stronger material than wood, size for size, which means that the individual pieces of the structure can be more slender. This allows better light admission for the same strength. It also needs virtually no treatment or maintenance. Modern designs are extremely clever, following all the work that has been done on stresses and strains, so that a minimum of material is needed for them to be stable. This is reflected in the modern design of greenhouses where the standard size of glass is now 24in square, as opposed to 20in, which it was previously.

The interior of the greenhouse.

The downside of an aluminium frame with acrylic glazing is that the whole thing can end up next door in a gale, so it needs to be well anchored. This is one good reason for having glass instead of 'plastic' for glazing; it adds weight and, therefore, stability. It is also another reason for making sure that the site is sheltered.

Aluminium is certainly the 'material of the moment' and many more domestic greenhouses are made of aluminium rather than wood. It is also easy to carry home, straightforward to put up, needs very little maintenance and gives better light admission. However, until about the 1960s, wood ruled. Teak was originally favoured

for making greenhouses because of its low maintenance requirements, but its cost was comparatively high and it gave way to Western Red Cedar (*Thuja plicata*). This has been the standard timber for making good greenhouses for a long time and remains so. It has everything: strength, durability and lightness. The only disadvantage is that it needs cleaning and treating with a preservative every few years. Wood has a more 'homely' feel and is better looking. It is also more versatile, and can be drilled, nailed or pinned if anything needs to be attached to the frame.

Deal is a cheaper alternative but its useful life is less than that of *Thuja* and, for this reason, it needs more frequent cleaning and treating.

Painting wooden greenhouses white is beneficial in two main respects. Its preservative properties ensure that the wood has a long life and it is better than unpainted wood at reflecting light. White paint is the best for reflecting light (and therefore heat) in the summer and increasing the brightness of the structure in winter.

Other materials for building greenhouses have been tried over the years but all have fallen by the wayside, for one reason or another. Even concrete was considered, but the wider glazing bars necessary cut out more winter light than was acceptable. The internal iron strengthening rods were also a weakness as they were likely to rust more than was acceptable.

The floor of this greenhouse is of lain, used bricks.

IN-BUILT FEATURES

The Floor

Most people hardly give a thought to the floor of a greenhouse and simply leave it untouched, as uneven, stamped-down soil, or whatever else it might be. That is acceptable, but it is not very conscientious or practical. For a start, it is likely to be wet or even muddy during the winter. It will very likely be colonized by weeds and, while this is not a disaster, it will add a general air of damp and decay to the whole set-up. There is also a risk of weeds harbouring pests and diseases that could spread to the rightful occupiers of the greenhouse.

The best floor surface is porous and absorbent, to keep the greenhouse more or less dry and, therefore, pleasant. During the summer, it will be a constant source of moisture, which will help to keep the plants cool and damp. Old red bricks are ideal for ground covering: they are generally free, or at least cheap, they are absorbent but allow surplus water to drain away between them, and they look good. The overall effect is 'informal'. This style may also be achieved with shingle.

Paving slabs are certainly clean and tidy but they may take a bit of fiddling to get them to fit if they are supplied in a certain size. In other words, the floor has to fit the slabs. Bricks and paving slabs are best bedded on to sand so that they do not wobble, and the natural surface below must be beaten firm and level before laying the sand.

Finally, concrete is probably the most permanent and trouble-free type of flooring, and best for a large greenhouse, where bricks and slabs would take far too long to put down and would be too fiddly a job on such a scale.

Staging

Wooden staging can be seen in the picture below. The flooring can go down last of all, after putting in the staging and levelling off its 'legs'. Wobbly staging is very frustrating. If the staging is not on a firm base at this point, try to make it level by putting a brick or tile under every leg. Unless it is essential to cover it, the ground under the staging is best left bare as it will provide a lot of atmospheric moisture during the summer. Interestingly, you will often find seedlings growing under the staging that are difficult to grow from seed in a more orthodox way. Nature sometimes does better without any intervention.

One important decision is whether to have staging on both sides of the greenhouse or on one side only (preferably the south-facing side), or to have none at all. This will largely depend on what is going to be grown in the greenhouse.

The most popular practice is to have staging on one side and a 'border' on the other. In this way, bedding plants and so on that are wanted for outdoors at home can be raised in the greenhouse, along with pot plants for the house. There will still be ample room for tomatoes, cucumbers and other tall greenhouse vegetables and flowers planted in or standing on the border.

Staging made of wooden slats is low-cost and serviceable, and allows good air circulation.

If, however, it is unlikely that the border is going to be used either for planting and growing or for housing large plants in grow-bags, then it might be more practical to have staging on both sides.

If the greenhouse is to be used mainly as a propagating house for raising half-hardy plants for outside, then it could be more appropriate to have as much staging as can be fitted in. After all, these plants will spend only a comparatively short time under glass and the vast majority will be in pots before being moved outside for hardening off or and/or planting.

If there are several 'growing' (as opposed to propagating) houses and a particular one is going to be used mainly for propagating, then it could be wise to go a stage further and have more, narrower, staging suspended from the roof. To avoid overloading, only the lightweight plants should be kept on this upper 'storey'.

There are various types of staging. Many manufacturers of greenhouses supply the slatted wooden type when the greenhouse is bought. This is a good system and very convenient for a mixed greenhouse. It is first-rate for plants growing in all kinds of container and also for seedlings, and so on, in seed trays. An aluminium greenhouse will be supplied with aluminium staging and it is hard to think of anything better. Slatted staging (wood or aluminium) is light, it does not stay wet for long and its design allows air to pass through it so that the plants on it are kept well aired. Aluminium, especially, lasts a long time and, if it needs to be moved, this can be done without a major upheaval.

The life of wooden staging will be greatly extended if it is scrubbed clean and treated with an appropriate preservative

A large, general-purpose conservatory designed for displaying ornamentals both in containers and planted in the ground.

every couple of years or so. Makers of greenhouses usually supply staging with the greenhouse for just one side, but it may be possible to do a deal with the seller.

Sometimes, usually in 'display' greenhouses or display benches in mixed houses, sand or gravel is used in large aluminium or plastic trays placed on the staging. The trays, complete with wet sand or gravel, and plants in pots, can be a terrific weight. An aluminium house is clearly ideal as it is

In a small greenhouse, this capillary irrigation tray saves a lot of watering. The tray is watertight and the white Perlite holds the water that is absorbed by the compost through the holes in the base of the pots.

stronger, longer-lasting and easier to keep clean. Using reasonably fine sand, this is often the only system used in large display houses as it reduces enormously the amount of hand- or hose-watering that has to be done. These benches are often called 'capillary' or 'irrigation' benches.

Guttering and Drainage

Obviously, in a greenhouse, the outside rainfall is of no direct use to the plants. That does not stop it falling, though, and most of that which falls on the roof has to be led away somewhere. This is the main purpose of guttering. It also stops rainwater from running down the sides of the building and rotting the wood, if applicable. Guttering should preferably be made of plastic or aluminium, and pressed galvanized steel is also fine. In the past, guttering was made of cast iron, which often outlived the greenhouse but would be far too heavy for today's garden greenhouses.

If it is directed into a metal or plastic tank, rainwater can be stored and used afterwards for can-watering the plants in the greenhouse and elsewhere near by. Preferably, this tank should be inside the greenhouse, if possible sunk in the ground at one end of the house, so that the water is kept at 'greenhouse' temperature, for the benefit of the plants. An inside tank is especially helpful for winter watering, when the water could be frozen solid in an outside tank. The best place is in the gloom under the staging, where the formation of algae in the water will be discouraged.

An outside tank will need a lid, to stop rubbish blowing in and algae and green 'seaweed' forming in the water. A lid will be doubly important if the tank is inside and sunk in the ground under the staging, where a lot of rubbish from the staging will fall into it.

If it is not to be sunken, a purpose-made garden water tank with a low-down tap on the side at the bottom will do very well. Do not be tempted to pick up some Heath Robinson-style set-up from a scrapyard; they seldom save money and are always as bad as they look. It is simple to place a proper plastic or fibreglass water butt against the greenhouse under the downpipe from the guttering, but it must be raised on a stand of bricks of a suitable height so that a watering can will fit under the tap for filling. This must be done right at the start because, once the tank is full, it weighs a ton and cannot be moved.

Ventilation

The most important part of a greenhouse is its ventilation system. Anyone can build a greenhouse so that the inside temperature is higher than the outside – indeed, a simple cloche will provide that environment – but close control of the temperature is a more complicated issue. Different groups of plants require different amounts of heat, and plants will not want to be baked during the day and frozen at night. Some families of plants will put up with it, but that does not mean that they like it. For example, cacti will tolerate a life of extremes but they would rather not have to.

Most greenhouse manufacturers, understanding that hot air rises, put ventilators at the highest point – in the ridge of the house. It is a good idea, but it is only half the story. Certainly there should be ridge vents, to let out the hottest air, which has risen to the ridge of the house. However, that does very little to reduce the temperature of the air around the plants, which will be sitting either on the ground or, more likely, on waist-high staging. It is vital, therefore, to have ventilators along the sides of the greenhouse, at the same height as the staging. These side vents will allow cool air from outside to be drawn into the house as the hot air disappears through the ridge vents, resulting in fresh air passing among the plants; cooling them very effectively.

The normal type of side vent is hinged at the top and swings outwards. The alternative is the louvre type, which is said to give better air circulation. A greenhouse that is not fitted with side vents is not a good greenhouse. It indicates that the designer may have cut corners to reduce costs, and has only a limited understanding of what is necessary.

Of course, all greenhouses have a door, but leaving it open will simply provide a 'hole' for cool air to be drawn in, regardless of whether or not it passes among the plants on the staging.

The door will be either hinged or sliding. There is very little to choose between them and both can be partially opened to help with ventilation. As long as an outward-swinging door can open without catching on the ground, which can usually be arranged, it is very much a question of taking what comes. An inward-swinging door will be opening over levelled ground, so there should be no problem. It should have a hook to hold it open; if it does not, then it is worth fitting one.

With larger greenhouses, the doors should be wide enough to allow a wheelbarrow to pass through. This will be a great help when shifting bags of compost or moving plants in and out. Larger greenhouses usually have sliding doors.

MAKING THE PURCHASE

In the last couple of decades, the greenhouse market has changed beyond all recognition, both in terms of what is available and where the items can be bought, from the more traditional garden centres and DIY stores to the bigger supermarkets. It is worth taking plenty of time to look at what is available, consulting catalogues, researching online, visiting garden centres and asking questions. Gardening magazines are also full of helpful advice.

2 Setting up the Greenhouse

COOLING

Ventilation

Temperature is the single most important factor about a greenhouse and it has to be mastered right from the start. Of the two extremes, stopping a greenhouse from getting too hot in the summer is much the more important. As long as the temperature is above freezing, most of the plants that are going to be grown will stand a surprising amount of cold for a short time, by simply 'shutting down'. On the other hand, excessive heat will quickly upset them.

Heading the list of desirable gadgets would be one or more automatic ventilator openers; the number really depends on the

An 'alpine' house used for growing plants and bulbs whose natural habitat is mountainous; cold and dry winters and hot, sunny summers. The aim of the alpine house is to replicate these conditions. The side vents at bench height keep the plants cold and dry during the winter. At the same time, good ventilation discourages winter fungal diseases, such as Botrytis.

size of the greenhouse but it is wiser to err on the generous side, in proportion to their cost. Automatic openers are a godsend to both the gardener and the plants. The gardener will be relieved of the duty to get up in the small hours of a sunny June morning to open the ventilators before the sun raises the temperature to a volcanic height, and an automatic ventilator will also be a vital asset while the gardener is away on holiday. The plants will be protected from the roller-coaster temperature variations that otherwise exist, which are always to their detriment.

Most automatic openers operate very simply on oil that expands or contracts in a cylinder when the temperature rises or falls. This change in volume is usually transmitted

Not all large greenhouses are built with specific plants in mind. This is a general-purpose house that is used for propagating plants destined for growing outdoors, as well as inside, and as a display house for tender ornamentals and vegetables (tomatoes, cucumbers, and so on).

mechanically via a rod attached to the ventilator. By lengthening or shortening the rod, the temperature at which the vent opens and closes can be altered. It is foolproof and seems not to need any attention except for the odd squirt of oil on the moving parts in the spring when it starts to work again after its winter rest. Its working life is virtually unlimited.

Even with the ventilators fully open, a greenhouse is quite likely to overheat, so it is a good idea to get into the habit of leaving the door open and on the hook at appropriate times.

Staying on the subject of keeping cool, another gadget that it is hard to do without is a fan heater that can be run with the the heating element on or off. Although this is primarily for heating, it is just as handy for cooling. It can be kept hanging by the door during the summer, so that it draws cooling air into the greenhouse. This, in conjunction with the top and side vents, makes sure that the temperature inside and outside the house is roughly the same, which should be the target in the summer.

It is not a question of allowing the greenhouse to be run entirely by gadgets – that would eliminate some of the fun of the actual 'gardening' – but the combination of vent openers and a hot/cold blower is an enormous help without actually taking any of the skill out of the hobby. They can always be turned off or disengaged when they are not needed.

Shading

Shading is another important way of keeping a greenhouse cool and, at the same time, preventing plants from being scorched by the sun. The most significant thing to remember about any system of shading is that it that it works more effectively if it is on the *outside* of the greenhouse. It is possible to buy roll-up shading to be fitted to the *inside* of a greenhouse. This is excellent for keeping the sun off the plants, and thereby avoiding sun scorch, and it does, of course, reduce the temperature inside the greenhouse a bit. However, because it does not prevent the actual rays of the sun (and therefore its heat) from coming in, it is only partially effective. Its main benefit is that it is easy to put up and manage.

The most effective method of shading has, for many years, been whitewash on the outside of the glass. This fulfils the main objective of greenhouse shading, by stopping the rays of the sun from entering the greenhouse. It does, though, present a number of drawbacks. First, once it is on the glass, it is there until it is scrubbed off in the autumn – whether it is needed or not. Fortunately, when it is properly applied, it is not so dense as to create a gloomy interior during cloudy weather. Its application can also be extremely messy. If a garden sprayer is used for this, everything in the vicinity can end up covered with whitewash. And if the vents are not closed, even the plants will be covered!

There are several makes, all based on roughly the same principle. The more sophisticated versions change their degree of transparency with the weather. The 'whitewash' type can equally be used on glass cloches and cold frames. There is no limit to the size or shape of the structure that can be treated.

For convenience and cost, the most universal kinds of shading are the green plastic sort, usually woven. Extruded polythene, or something similar, cuts out about 50 per cent of the sunlight, and is conveniently flexible when the weather it warm, though it does become a bit less easy to handle when the weather is cold and grey. It is attached to the outside of the greenhouse and can be cut to the shape and size that it is wanted. In the autumn it can be rolled up and stored until it is needed again in the spring. It is held in place with push-pins of a suitable size (another benefit of having a wooden frame).

As an alternative, there is a woven, thin, green, plastic raffia-like material, which is sold in rolls in garden centres. This is more flexible, in both senses, and easier to handle than the extruded material but possibly not quite as easy to put on the greenhouse (and keep it there) when it is windy. Again, push-pins hold it in place.

These two types of plastic material will certainly last for five to ten years before they start to break down and get brittle.

The best shading product is a blind-like structure of thin, wooden strips, about the thickness of a split cane, that are 'sown' together. This can be raised and lowered as the need arises, over a frame attached to the outside of the greenhouse, using ropes and pullies. This type of product is at the top of the market as far as appearance, efficiency and cost are concerned.

The time of year when shading should be put on a greenhouse will vary with every year. This is why the whitewash version is not ideal – it is either on or off. With the roll-up shading, it is much easier to take it off or put it on again as the weather dictates.

Damping Down

Water may also be used for keeping plants cool. The best way is to 'damp down' the plants from above, spraying over them with a hose. This is best done either with a fine rose on the hose or by nipping the end. Alternatively, a watering can with a fine rose is perfect on a small scale.

The practice of damping down the plants from above when the sun is actually out is sometimes frowned upon, but the potential damage is over-stated. It may not be a good idea in conditions of extreme heat but in any case action should be taken before such conditions arise.

Overhead damping down is the quickest and most effective way of reducing the temperature of the leaf surface and, therefore, reducing the risk of dehydration and scorch. It also brings down the temperature within the greenhouse, which is its main purpose.

Watering the floor of the greenhouse will also have a cooling effect. Water lying on bricks, slabs, or even an earth floor, is enormously effective at cooling the whole interior.

Heating

Even the most economically minded greenhouse owner, experienced or novice, will want to heat their greenhouse. An unheated greenhouse is perfectly satisfactory for a beginner and, indeed, many experienced gardeners have a 'cold house' for growing alpines and other plants and bulbs that require very little additional warmth in the winter. Heat becomes useful when the greenhouse is required for raising young plants during the spring. In the summer and early autumn, the warmth of the sun will normally be ample for raising new plants, whether they are destined for staying under cover or for going outside.

However, to get the maximum use and enjoyment from a greenhouse, even a minimum of 'artificial' heat will make all the difference. Even keeping it just frost-free in the winter considerably widens the range of plants that can be grown.

The first and most important point is that the heater must be big enough to heat the greenhouse. If the greenhouse is larger than average, it may be necessary to have two heaters, to be on the safe side. Knowing the greenhouse dimensions when buying a heater avoids a wasted journey. Electric heaters, for example, will nearly always carry a recommendation for the maximum size of greenhouse that they will heat economically. In other words, if a heater is too small, it may not do the job unless it is running at maximum output the whole time.

Coal- and Coke-Fired Systems

In the past, all greenhouses, no matter what their size, were heated by a coal- or coke-fired boiler, usually in a pit below ground level. These systems are still to be found in some of the oldest (usually Victorian) walled gardens. The boiler supplied the energy to heat the water, which was then circulated round the greenhouse in cast-iron pipes. There were no circulation pumps and the water flowed because, by convection, the hot water pushed round the water that was cooling. The hot water left the top of the boiler and passed into the pipes, where it lost heat into the greenhouse. The cooler water that it was pushing round returned to the bottom of the boiler to be re-heated, and so on. It was a cumbersome system that needed constant attention to keep the fire going, but it did have one benefit that modern systems do not have: the comparatively large amount of water cooled quite slowly and, therefore, maintained a reasonably high temperature for a considerable time even if the fire went out (the equivalent of a power cut stopping

the circulation pump working). Today a system like this would be fitted only as part of a restoration project, as its operation would be far too labour-intensive.

The aim today is still fundamentally the same as it was in the past: to heat the air inside the greenhouse so that the plants growing in it have a warmer environment. That may be because they need it to survive, as in the case of plants from warmer countries, or it could be to advance the growth of plants whose normal season of growth outdoors in their native country is naturally later in the year. This would normally involve out-of-season crops such as forcing bulbs or growing winter lettuces but it can also be extended to include the raising of, say, half-hardy bedding plants for planting outside.

Paraffin Heaters

The simplest source of heat, and the one with which countless generations of gardeners have started, is one that runs on paraffin. The stove must be one that it designed for use in a greenhouse and a garden centre is certainly the best place to go for it. The heater must be a 'blue flame burner', made to burn with a blue flame, not a partially yellow one. The blue flame indicates that the heater is operating efficiently and at a higher temperature than one which burns with a yellow or yellow/blue flame. If most or all of the flame is yellow, the stove is operating at a lower temperature than it should be, and not all the paraffin is burning completely. This, in turn, will lead to paraffin vapour in the greenhouse, which will certainly damage some, if not all, the plants. A strong smell of partially burnt paraffin is a sure sign of trouble.

If an existing stove, which normally burns with a blue flame, changes to a flame that is part blue and part yellow, it is likely that the wick needs cleaning and/or trimming. If this fails to correct the problem, a new wick may be the answer.

It is worth mentioning that certain plants, notably ferns, are never happy in a greenhouse where there is a paraffin heater, no matter how well it is working. At best, it can make them look sickly; at worst, it may cause the leaves to turn brown and die.

The only other point about a paraffin heater is that there should always be a can of paraffin handy, although certainly not in the greenhouse, for refilling the stove. If it runs out of fuel on the coldest night of the year, it is a hard-learned lesson. Keep the can in a safe place and refill it as soon as it is empty. Also, remember that stoves may need topping up, and certainly looking at, every day during a cold spell.

Some greenhouse paraffin heaters have a metal 'dish' on top in which to put water to stop the atmosphere in the greenhouse getting too dry. This is unnecessary. In fact, it is counter-productive, as paraffin heaters tend to create a damp atmosphere anyway. It is good practice to leave a chink of ventilation when a paraffin heater is running, to allow some air circulation. This will avoid the induced dampness.

Bottled Gas Heaters

A step up from a paraffin heater is one that is fuelled by bottled gas, normally propane/butane. These are relatively cheap to run and are efficient. Some are even fitted with a thermostat to keep a steady temperature. They also create a damper atmosphere than is desirable so, again, it is wise to keep on a chink of ventilation when they are in use.

This electric fan heater is top of the list for cleanliness, efficiency and ease of use. This normally outweighs the slightly higher running cost.

When properly set, a bottled-gas heater should not emit any harmful gases. Its worst fault will probably be that it is heavy and cumbersome.

It is a good idea to buy a model fitted with a pressure gauge; those without one can run out of gas without warning.

Electrical Heaters

Electrical heaters are at the top end of the range and, for a small greenhouse, they cannot be bettered. They are 'clean', in that they give off no harmful fumes; in fact, there is no reason why they should not be used indoors.

Avoid one that is not thermostatically controlled – in this case, a cheaper machine

29

will cost more to run than a more expensive one. Indeed, some of the best small models cost little more to run than a light bulb. Electrical tubular heaters also work well and are surprisingly efficient to run. However, a fan heater is to be preferred because it can double for a fan cooler in the summer, with the heating element turned off.

Of course, electricity will be needed to run this type of heater and this brings in another point about electrically driven gadgets: their vulnerability to power cuts, which nearly always occur during the winter, when the heater is at its busiest. Despite this drawback, there is no question about the importance of electricity in a greenhouse.

INSULATION

Heating a greenhouse is only half the story. Just as important is keeping the heat in, and not wasting it. Whatever is done, heat is going to escape. However, certain steps can be taken that will greatly reduce the loss. The first and most obvious one is keeping the ventilators closed. Fitting vents with an automatic opening device goes a long way towards keeping an even temperature in the greenhouse. In the same way, they will keep hot air in the greenhouse on a cold day by staying closed.

There will come a time when the air is so much colder outside the greenhouse than inside that heat will escape directly through the glass. Putting a membrane, such as polythene sheeting, on the inside of the glass creates two layers (polythene and glass) through which the heat has to escape, instead of just one (glass). However, there is a price to pay. Ventilation will be impeded such that condensation will form on the inside of the glass. In the winter this will lead to a damp atmosphere, which, in turn, will encourage

During the winter, one way of helping to keep the heat in, so that the heater is not running perpetually, is to fix bubble plastic to the inside of the house. In a wooden house this can be fixed with drawing pins. On a metal frame, sticky tape is normally the answer, although there are a number of gadgets that can be used, depending on the make of the house. Bubble plastic will make the house virtually airtight, which can lead to excessive dampness. This, in turn, will increase the risk of Botrytis (grey mould). It is always a good idea, therefore, to open the door on suitable occasions during the winter to give an air change and reduce the risk of fungal disease. If Botrytis does become a problem, it is often better to remove the bubble plastic and rely on spending more on heating. It may also be a good idea to leave the roof vents uncovered and open them whenever suitable.

Botrytis (grey mould), one of the most damaging fungus diseases.

Bubble polythene lessens the problem but the real solution is either to have the vents uncovered, so that they can work normally, or to cover them with the polythene and then cut round them so that they can still be used as ventilators. The three-sided flap of polythene that you cut round the vents can be drawing-pinned to wooden vents or stuck to the metal with sticky tape, if the house is aluminium.

There is another benefit to covering the vents with polythene and then cutting it. It allows the ventilators to be opened and closed for temperature control. Full ventilation should be given occasionally, on sunny days, regardless of the outside temperature, to clean out the old, stale, damp air and replace it with new.

WATERING

Hoses and Watering Cans

In the past, one common way of watering pot plants was to use a lance about 45cm (18in) long, with a rose on the end attached to a hose. The rose was generally 5cm (2in) wide at the most, but generally less. Today, it seems impossible to find a metal, or even a plastic rose of this size. With the smaller rose, individual pots can be watered very easily. Of course, the bigger one will do the job more quickly, but everything in sight will be soaked, whether it needs to be or not.

A lance on the end of the hose is vital where the staging or benches are wide. It is the only way of watering pot plants on the far side of the staging without soaking everything. It also prevents the pots being knocked off the staging by a stretching arm.

A purpose-made watering lance may have an on/off tap and at least one rose, and ideally two – a fine one and a coarse one. If it proves difficult to track one down in a garden centre, the best solution is to buy a length of aluminium tubing about 60cm (2ft) long and of a diameter to fit tightly inside the end of the hose, and use a little ingenuity.

Historically, garden hoses were made of one layer of rubber and, more recently, of flexible plastic. The problem with this construction is that they kink. The single layer of rubber or plastic is not enough for the hose to hold its shape and, the moment it is bent, such as when turning a corner, it develops a kink. This is quickly followed by an increase in pressure within the hose and, inevitably, something has to give. Normally, the end attached to the tap flies off and soaks everything. In addition, these hoses are also difficult to coil up tidily on the ground. Their only virtue is that they are cheap, and rightly so. In a greenhouse, they are an abomination. They are at their worst in winter when the water is cold and the hose is stiff. Fortunately, this is also when they are least used; it is often as easy to use a watering can instead.

The best modern hoses are of layered construction: two or three layers of rubber or flexible plastic with nylon mesh, or something similar, between the layers. Rubber was originally used but plastic has taken over and the life of a hose is now infinitely longer than it used to be.

Hoses are usually available in three different diameters: half-inch, three-quarters of an inch and one inch. For the average home greenhouse, the half-inch is fine, as it carries as much water as is normally needed while remaining manageable. A 25-metre hose of this kind will cost about £30.

The usual alternative to mains water is a watering can, but this is entirely up to personal preference. Haws have made the best watering cans for years. They may be the most expensive (around £40–£50) but, properly looked after, they will easily last one or even two lifetimes. Haws also have a cheaper range, which vary in terms of design, colour, finish and material, and have interchangeable coarse and fine, round and oval roses. Their highest-quality cans are galvanized or painted brick-red. The capacities range from 6 pints (3.5 litres) through 1 gallon (4.5 litres) to 2 gallons (8.8 litres). The best watering can for greenhouse work is a 'long-reach' can, with a long spout that is ideal for reaching to the back of the staging.

The two most obvious sources of water for a greenhouse are the mains and collected rainwater, but there are other sources. In the outdoor garden, more or less any water can safely be used, as long as it is not too filthy. However, in the greenhouse, and indeed wherever plants are in containers, inside or out, it is important to be rather more choosy. There is nothing intrinsically wrong with 'second-hand' water but solids within that water could build up in potting compost and clog up its air spaces. This could ultimately lead to the compost becoming waterlogged in the containers and, finally, killing the plants. This is an extreme case but it is a possibility.

Some second-hand water, such as bath water, is full of chemicals that are 'organic', in the broadest sense of the word. Obviously this is not the sort of organic matter that goes on the compost heap, but it is organic, none the less, and before long

will start to decompose and go smelly. The oil in soap is probably the main offender. In garden beds and borders, these materials will be 'diluted' in the soil and broken down by micro-organisms, to the extent that they become completely benign. In containers, however, they cannot escape. Bath water is harmless when it is reused in the open garden among the flower beds and vegetables, but not in the greenhouse.

Much the same can be said about the soapy 'washing' water that comes out of a washing machine, which, with its detergent and dirt, is not suitable for reuse. It would be acceptable to use the 'rinse' water, but its use must not be overdone.

In a greenhouse, though, the advice is to stick to mains or rainwater. Some gardeners are concerned about the additives to tap water, such as chlorine, but none of these is present in sufficient strength to have any detrimental effect on plants.

There is one important exception to using tap water to water plants: where the mains water is naturally chalky/limey, it should not be used on 'ericaceous' (lime-hating) plants in containers, either under cover or in the open. These plants include azaleas, camellias, heathers, rhododendrons, skimmia and a few other less common ones. These must be watered with rainwater as the limey tap water will partially prevent them absorbing certain plant nutrients.

If there is access to a river or stream, as long as the land through which it flows is not chalk or limestone, the water should be perfectly safe for watering all plants. There is no such thing as a certainty in gardening, however, so it is worth asking a neighbour or running a small trial with half a dozen plants before submitting the whole lot to it.

'Automatic' Watering Systems

A pot plant indoors is usually stood in a saucer. When watering, water is poured on to the compost until it starts to run out of the bottom of the pot, which normally indicates that the compost is fully moist. Over the next couple of days, the plant will absorb water from the compost. As the plant continues to take up water, the compost will start to dry out, and will replace its lost water by absorbing any that is in the saucer. The process – the natural movement of water from a wet medium to a drier one – is called 'capillary action'. A plant's roots use the same action to absorb water from the compost.

The scale of this process can be enlarged by creating a 'capillary bench' in the greenhouse. Put an aluminium or plastic tray, about 90cm (3ft) square, on the staging and fill it level full with fine sand. As many as fifty pot plants are then placed firmly on the sand, and given a little twist to make sure that the compost in the pot is in contact with the sand. Water is added carefully until the sand is completely saturated, but there is no free water standing above the surface of the sand. This is a system that is used commercially and in large greenhouses where the high number of pot plants makes hand-watering uneconomical.

The bench should be checked every day and, when the sand is seen to be drying out, water should be added, using a watering can with a rose. This makes less of a mess of the sand surface, which can lead to uneven watering. Plant nutrients can also be given in this way, simply by applying dilute feed to the sand in place of plain water. Alternatively, the feed can be applied straight to the actual pots so that there is no doubt that they have been fed.

For another semi-automatic watering system, arrange an up-turned gallon bottle of water so that the open top of the bottle is firmly on the wet surface of the sand. As the sand dries out, the airtight join between the wet sand and the water in the bottle will be broken. This will allow air into the bottle and as a result water will seep into the sand. This set-up is not usually suitable for administering feed.

It can be expanded in a reasonably large greenhouse by having a 20-gallon airtight tank full of water located above the height of the benching, with a hosepipe connecting it to the sand. As the sand dries out, the end of the hosepipe will no longer be under the water creating an airtight seal, air will get into the tank and sufficient water will be released to re-wet the sand. When the saturation level reaches the bottom end of the hosepipe, the seal will be re-established and no more water will be released from the tank.

There are a number of manufacturers offering watering and irrigation equipment, and many types of system can be rigged up, using a little ingenuity. One idea that is splendid for the amateur greenhouse owner, involves an appropriate length of 'leaky hose' laid on the sand of a capillary bench, with the other end attached to the mains tap. When the tap is turned on slightly, water runs into the hose and, thence, into the sand. The tap is simply turned off once the sand is as moist as it needs to be.

Where grow-bags, large pots and/or containers are on one or both sides of the greenhouse, it is relatively easy to set up a trickle irrigation system. It is more or less the same as the system using the 'leaky hose', with an ordinary hose and a nozzle supplying each pot or bag.

Misting and Mist Propagation

The time will come when a packet of seeds and hardwood cuttings of forsythia seem too elementary and the urge will come to undertake some slightly more advanced plant propagation. The next step is to take some 'semi-ripe' cuttings, which is the method by which most shrubs are propagated. Cuttings are taken in mid- to late summer, when the plants will shortly stop growing. These are usually 'terminal' cuttings, the leafy top 5–8cm (2–3in) of a shoot cut off immediately below a leaf. Semi-ripe cuttings can also comprise short side shoots (again 5–8cm (2–3in) long), with a 'heel' of older wood at the base. The base of each cutting is inserted a 50/50 mix of peat (or substitute) and sharp sand in a pot or seed tray. They will root quite easily if the pot is carefully put into a polythene bag and the top then turned over and held shut with a paper clip. This will create a 'closed circuit' within the bag, with the moisture going round and round from the compost to the cuttings to the atmosphere as water vapour, and back to the compost as 'condensation', with none escaping.

A misting unit being used to water young bedding plants in a propagating house.

Where several pots or trays of cuttings are involved, it is more convenient to keep them moist by putting them under a 'mist propagator'. It is easy to make a simple one, either in a corner of a capillary bench but more often in a small sand tray of, say, 40–60cm (16–24in) square. A mist propagator consists, quite simply, of a fine misting nozzle on a rod, which keeps it about 30cm (12in) above the bench. The rod is attached to the water supply pipe. On a commercial scale, an electronic 'leaf' is placed among the cuttings and connected to a control box through a low-voltage electric cable. On its upper, flat, disc-like surface are two brass contact plates, each less than 1cm (half an inch) in diameter and not touching each other. A two-core electric wire is already attached to the 'leaf', one wire to each contact plate, and the other end of the wire goes into the control box. The mains water and the electricity are then switched on and, because the two contact points on the 'leaf' are not connected to each other, either physically or by water, a valve in the control box opens and water flows through, under pressure, to the misting nozzle. This showers very small water droplets on to anything beneath it. After a second or two, the two contact plates are connected by a thin film of water and the valve in the control box cuts off the water supply. A minute or two later, the water on the 'leaf' dries out, the low-level current stops flowing between the contacts and the water cuts in again; and so on. . . . It is perfectly simple but brilliant at the job for which it is intended. To use this device as a plant propagator, the cuttings are simply placed in the sand bed beneath the mister. The average 'throw' of the nozzle is in a circle about 60cm (2ft) across.

To go a step further and create a self-contained propagator, make a shallow 'frame' out of four bits of wood, each 60cm (2ft) long by 20cm (8in) wide. The thickness does not really matter, as it is not going to be load-bearing; anything round 2–3cm (about an inch) is fine. With a sheet of Perspex or polythene resting on the wooden edges, there really is no need for anything else.

An extension of this is to have a full-time mister taking care of watering all the pot plants on either ordinary staging or above a capillary bench. If this is to be used above slatted staging, the staging should be in aluminium rather than wood, which would soon rot if not properly maintained.

The other vital component in plant propagation is warmth and this can be achieved by burying soil-warming cables in the peat/sand rooting medium in the floor of the propagator. These can be bought together with a thermostat and control box.

Any queries arising during the setting up of these units should be addressed to one of the specialist manufacturers in equipment used for irrigation, watering and/or misting.

All this may sound unnecessary but an experienced and knowledgeable gardener will use all the modern techniques and methods available in order to eliminate the element of luck from plant propagation. Warmth, moisture and light at a constant level are all necessary for cuttings to develop roots quickly. The quicker a cutting forms roots, the less likely it is to die. The amount of moisture lost by the cuttings when a mister is used is virtually nil, and that is a very good reason for including such a system.

FEEDING PLANTS

The Essential Elements

Feeding is the other essential and regular job that has to be done to make sure that the plants in the greenhouse stay alive and prosper. To stay strong and healthy, the vast majority of plants need a 'diet' containing twelve essential elements, in varying amounts. These are divided into six 'major' elements and six 'trace' elements. The latter were originally referred to as 'minor' elements, which might suggest that they are less important. In fact, they are just as important as the major elements; the only difference is that they are required in much smaller quantities.

Of the major elements, the three that are most familiar to gardeners are nitrogen, phosphorus and potassium, which are required in the greatest quantities. The twelve elements are often referred to by their chemical symbol; nitrogen, phosphorus and potassium are N, P and K, respectively; the other three major elements are calcium (Ca), magnesium (Mg) and sulphur (S). The six trace elements are boron (Bo), manganese (Mn), iron (Fe), copper (Cu), zinc (Zn) and molybdenum (Mo).

The elements perform certain jobs, both individually and in combination, and a deficiency in any of the elements can cause a plant to look rather sickly. The reason for a lack of performance can usually be ascertained by a process of elimination: once an attack by pests or disease, and frost, drought and other natural disasters have been ruled out, the diagnosis is likely to be a mineral deficiency.

It is not vital to determine exactly which single element, or combination of the twelve essential elements, is in short supply, since many of the liquid feeds available contain

35

all, or most of, the essential major elements, as well as many of the minor ones. This will be indicated on the packaging; any feeds that are of organic origin, such as seaweed or chicken manure, will certainly contain them all.

Because nitrogen is the element that is required in the greatest amounts by plants, it is also the element that is most likely to be in short supply when a plant is showing deficiency symptoms (lack of growth, paling of the leaves, lack of flowers, and so on). Also, it is very soluble in water so it is soon washed out of the soil or potting compost by rain and watering. Since it is likely to be in short supply more quickly than other elements, it is usually the one that is included in the highest quantity in proprietary feeds. Nitrogen is the element responsible for growth, so if some of the plants in a batch have practically stopped growing, a shortage of nitrogen it probably the cause.

Potassium, normally called 'potash', is the element that encourages flowering and, hence, fruiting. It is therefore more important to tomatoes and many other 'fruiting' and flowering plants than nitrogen.

When to Feed

The usual way of feeding greenhouse plants is to apply water-soluble feeds when watering. During the growing season, it is then possible to make a note to feed on a specific day of the week – one feed a week will be sufficient for virtually all plants – otherwise, it is all too easy to forget.

Feed is normally only given during the growing season, from about early spring to early autumn, when the plants need it most. In the early spring, plants will start

growing naturally; if they fail to do so on their own, they should be given a reminder in the form of some liquid feed. This will get them going. At the other end of the growing season, they need to be encouraged to have a rest and go dormant for the winter, so feeding is stopped and the temperature in the greenhouse is allowed to drop a little. The aim is to copy nature so that, when the days are shortening and the light is diminishing (and there is the consequent drop in temperature), growth is discouraged; as the days lengthen, the plants are encouraged to grow and/or flower again. If growth is encouraged during the winter, it will be weak and mainly useless.

Of course, feeding should be in proportion to watering so that, as watering is started, so feeding should begin; and vice versa in the autumn.

Methods of Feeding

Liquid feeds are most convenient for greenhouse plants because they can be incorporated into the vital job of watering. As in outdoor gardening, it is also possible to use granular fertilizers, which contain exactly the same nutrients. However, this does create a separate and extra job, and they do act less quickly than liquid feeds, because they have to be dissolved first and carried through the compost before the plants can show any response. Their application is also rather imprecise, which can lead to underfeeding or over-feeding.

If there are a significant number of plants to water and/or feed, it will be very time-consuming to keep mixing fresh batches of feed in a watering can. The answer to this problem is a 'hose-end diluter' or an 'in-hose diluter'. The difference between them is that the hose-end diluter is fitted to the delivery end of the watering hose whereas the in-hose type goes anywhere convenient along the hose, or actually at the tap. The two types work in exactly the same way: each has a reservoir filled with either soluble liquid feed crystals or liquid feed concentrate. The device meters this into the mains water running through the hose so that, whenever the hose and the diluter are turned on together, diluted feed is delivered at the correct strength. When the job is finished, the diluter is turned off and only plain water comes out of the hose.

With the in-hose diluter at the tap end, any other attachment, such as a lance or a different nozzle, can be fitted. A diluter attached to the delivery end of the hose is a more cumbersome set-up and plants can easily be knocked over on the staging. These diluters are sometimes sold together with the feed granules or liquid concentrate.

Feeding weekly through the growing season is a good general recommendation, but there is another new way of feeding plants in containers, with 'season-long' tablets of concentrated plant food. At the start of the growing season, one or more of the tiny tablets (about a centimetre or half an inch across) are pressed into the compost in the pot or container. Guidelines are given on the pack to show how many tablets are required for the different sizes of container. To avoid any double-dosing, containers and pots that have received their feed should be marked, perhaps with a small stick. An extra dose will not hurt the plants but it is wasteful and might cause excessive growth. Marking the pots also helps the gardener not to miss any out.

It is a very easy method, but, because the plants have to be watered anyway, there is perhaps little advantage in this type of feeding under glass.

Plants standing on a capillary bench are best fed with liquid feed from either a watering can or the diluter.

The super-forgetful who simply cannot remember on which day feeding is supposed to be carried out should turn down the diluter to half-strength and leave it like that throughout the summer. Weak feeding at every 'watering' will not hurt and is certainly better than no feeding at all.

DAY-LENGTH CONTROL AND SUPPLEMENTARY LIGHTING

By manipulating the amount of light in the greenhouse it is possible to 'tell' certain plants when to flower. This has been going on in commercial chrysanthemum greenhouses for fifty years and more, resulting in all-year-round (AYR) blooms. The time of year at which a plant flowers is governed by its genes and this mechanism can be used to alter the flowering time to suit the grower.

If everything were left to nature, different plants would flower at different times of the year, with each plant having its particular season. However, some plants are so popular that there is a market for them all year round. Chrysanthemums are the obvious example. As luck would have it, they are 'short-day' plants – they start flowering in the autumn when the days are getting shorter and, depending on the type and variety, will flower naturally until the longer days of spring stop them completely. By manipulating the conditions in which they are growing, their flowering time may be altered. To this end, they are either covered with a black polythene sheet, thus creating short days, ahead of when they are required to flower. Conversely, they can be artifically lit when it is desirable to delay flowering. A number of other considerations have to be taken into account, but that is the basic system.

The Christmas-flowering poinsettia is another plant that flowers during the UK's short days. To encourage it to flower again in its second UK winter, it must be subjected to sufficient darkness in the autumn. From the end of September, it must be covered with black polythene from the early evening until the following morning so that it experiences fourteen hours of darkness. After eight weeks of this it can go back to being treated normally. In other parts of the world this timetable would, of course, be modified accordingly. Even in an unlit greenhouse, the black polythene covering must be used; without it, even a street light can ruin the whole timetable and delay flowering.

The opposite of shading – supplementary lighting to increase day length in winter – is another complicated subject. Suffice it to say that there are many different models of lights suitable for use in greenhouses. It is important to use a purpose-made one and to remember that water and electricity do not mix.

COMPOSTS AND OTHER GROWING MEDIA

Development of Compost

The term 'medium' in this context refers to the material in which a plant's roots are growing. For plants that are growing in the ground, garden soil is the medium. For plants that are growing in a container of some sort – a pot, a trough, a seed tray, a grow-bag, and so on – the growing medium is probably one or other of the many manufactured materials.

In the past, the recipe for a professional horticulturist's own potting compost was a closely guarded secret, with the degree of secrecy reaching a ridiculous level; in some cases, the Head Gardener of a large estate would not allow even his own staff to know what went into the mixture. This state of affairs was accepted as normal until the

When potting up a young plant for the first time, or, later, when moving it into a larger pot because it has out-grown it's existing one (termed 'potting on'), use a compost of similar make up, to that of the original one, i.e. John Innes, peat-based, peat-free etc. The plant is used to growing in this kind of compost and changing it will often give the plant a check that it may take some time to overcome.

late 1940s, when the John Innes Institute decided to create a standardized product or material. Its make-up would be public knowledge so that, when a quantity was required somewhere, it could be bought by the gardener, estate, parks department, nursery, and so on, safe in the knowledge that it would be of a universal standard and make-up. This led to the birth of the world-famous John Innes range of composts.

Until the John Innes Institute began its work in earnest, 'compost' was simply the material made by gardeners at the bottom of the garden – the vegetative waste from the garden and/or kitchen, stored in a heap or special container so that it rotted down, over the space of a year or so, and could then be returned to the soil by being dug into the ground, usually during the winter. Introducing this material to the garden would improve the soil and subsequently benefit the plants put to grow in that soil.

The system is one of the oldest forms of recycling, but it plays no part in greenhouse gardening. To avoid confusion, most professionals tend to refer to the product of garden and kitchen waste 'garden compost'. The compost that interests the greenhouse gardener is, broadly speaking, called 'potting compost'.

When they are very young, plants require conditions that are different from those that they need during adolescence and adulthood. This relates both to the physical side of the material in which they are growing and to their nutrition, or their 'diet'. As a result, John Innes came up with both a Seed Compost, which was also suitable for cuttings, and a Potting Compost, which suited virtually all grown-up plants. Within a very short time, the potting compost was further split up into three 'versions', according to the amount of fertilizer that was required by plants of different age: John Innes Potting Compost 1, 2 and 3 (now referred to as JIP1, JIP2 and JIP3), with the number indicating their 'strength'.

The Sowing and Cuttings Compost is standard for everything. The physical make-up of the Seed Compost is peat and sharp sand. Both materials are easy enough to obtain and there is little variation, wherever they come from. The Potting Composts, however, are made up of peat, sharp sand and loam (soil), and it is via the loam element that difficulties can be encountered. As any gardener will know, soil can vary greatly from garden to garden. This led to research at the Institute, almost as soon as the JI composts became available, aimed at finding a way of excluding loam from the composts without sacrificing quality.

The USA was also in this race and, in the early 1960s, the University of California came up with a peat and sand compost, which they called 'UC Compost'. It was not a success as both the peat and the sand were far too fine and, in consequence, the compost was very difficult to wet. Once it was wet, it easily became water-logged. However, it was a valuable start.

In the UK, in the mid-1960s, Fisons launched its Levington Compost. Since then, many other brands have appeared and, today, virtually all sowing and potting composts are loam-free. Research at the moment is aimed at finding a suitable alternative to peat as the source of vegetative organic matter. It is an essential part of growing composts because it is the ingredient that absorbs and retains water and, at the same time, provides aeration; without which the compost would be useless.

Which Compost?

In the UK today, while the number of brands of potting compost is enormous, the number of actual producers is small, so there is very little to choose between any of them. The only substantial difference between them is whether or not they contain loam, so it more a matter of brand loyalty. There are, however, differences between potting composts and the composts that are used in grow-bags and those that are intended for use in pots, troughs, barrels and other containers. For this reason, they are not interchangeable. It is a false economy, for a number of reasons, to use compost out of a growbag in place of a branded potting compost on the basis of it costing less. Both are first rate at the job for which they are intended, but not for other purposes.

On the whole, it is best to find a compost that is comfortable to work with and seems to grow good plants, and stick with it. There is nothing to be gained by hopping about from one brand to another, chasing 'deals'.

As a general rule, 'permanent' pot plants in larger pots or troughs, tubs, and so on, which are either outside on a terrace or indoors in a living room, are happier in a loam-based compost. One reason for this is that this type of compost is heavier and, therefore, the plant will be more stable. Conversely, window boxes, hanging baskets and containers that hang on a wall will be better with a soil-less compost, so that they can be as light as possible.

Other Materials

Recently, coir has been used in soil-less composts, with a degree of success. It is made up of the partially ground-up husk of coconuts, so it is very light, and it is available in large quantities. However, its main disadvantage is that it does not hold water very well, so quickly dries out. While it holds water between its fibres against gravity, it does not actually absorb it into the fibres.

3 Plant Propagation

Plant propagation, whether by seed, cuttings or air layering, is a vital skill – it is, after all, how all plants start their life. Spring is certainly the best time for propagating greenhouse plants. This is when most seeds are sown and it is also common practice to take cuttings at this time too. The reason is simple. Spring propagation gives rooted cuttings, seedlings, and so on, the whole of the growing season in which to become established and independent before the lower temperatures and poorer light of autumn largely put a stop to growth. There are exceptions, but that is the general rule.

PROPAGATING FROM SEED

The simplest and most convenient way of producing new plants is from seed. This is the method by which the vast majority reproduce themselves naturally, with seed being produced sexually following the fertilization of a flower by pollen from another of the same species. Most young gardeners usually start growing plants by sowing vegetable seeds, such as peas and beans, in the veg plot. Such seeds are big and easy for little fingers to handle. Given the right conditions for germination and growth, seeds normally produce the quickest results, which is important in maintaining a child's interest. Seeds also represent the most productive method of propagation.

Greenhouse plants are normally sown in a suitable container, such as a flower pot or seed

Example of pot plants.

tray, using one of the composts. A 'seed compost' or a 'universal compost' are both suitable. The latter can be used both for raising new plants and for growing on existing ones, making it necessary to have only one compost rather than two.

Sowing lettuce seeds in the spring for germinating in the greenhouse. The resulting plants will be planted outdoors a month after sowing.

Filling a half-tray.

Gently firming down the compost.

Levelling the surface with a home-made presser.

Don't sow the seeds too thickly; this is about right.

Covering the seeds very shallowly with compost. The sieve will help you achieve an even covering and will also exclude any lumps in the compost. It can even be used when sowing to ensure the same.

Very gently pressing down the compost surface after sowing and covering.

This routine can also be followed with half-hardy vegetables, such as French and runner beans, which may be sown in pots in the greenhouse in mid-spring and planted outside when the risk of frost is over, four to six weeks later. These, though, are rather a special case and, more commonly, it is bedding plants and greenhouse ornamentals that are propagated in this way.

Using a suitably sized container for the quantity of seed that is to be sown, overfill the container with compost, roughly level it and press it down lightly with the fingers, especially round the sides. Strike it off level with the top of the container using a flat edge. Finally, after lightly firming the surface with an appropriately sized presser board, all is ready for sowing.

The most important thing during the filling and firming stage is not to press down the compost too much. Most of the composts consist of peat, or a peat substitute, which naturally holds a large amount of water. If the compost if over-firmed, it will hold more water than is required and will invariably lie wet. This will delay or even prevent germination and root growth.

Cut off the top of the seed packet and gently squeeze it to open it. Holding the open packet some 10–15cm (4–6in) above

Exacum, a member of the potato/tomato family, is a colourful little pot plant for the cool greenhouse or home. Its characteristic solanaceous flowers are carried throughout the summer and autumn. Grow from seed sown in spring.

Schizanthus has long been a popular and colourful plant for the cool greenhouse and the home. Individual plants are well worth growing though it is frequently used to fill in gaps in larger groups. If it has a fault, it is that it tends to attract red spider mite, which will soon stop it flowering and, ultimately, lead to defoliation.

the surface of the compost, tilt it until the seeds are on the point of spilling out. To get the seeds to fall out, use one finger to tap the side of the packet. Do not tilt the packet too much or the seeds will all come out with a rush and land in a heap. Holding the packet well above the compost will cause the seeds to bounce when they land on the surface and give a much more even distribution.

Once the seeds have been sown, sieve the same compost gently over them to bury them to about their own depth. Very small seeds, such as those of lobelia and begonias, should not be covered at all. After a final very gentle firming with the presser board, the whole thing is ready for watering. The best way to water the pot or seed tray is to stand it in a shallow container of water with the water coming about halfway up the sides, and no more. After a minute or two, the water will be seen to seep up through the surface of the compost and the pot or tray can be lifted out and stood at a slight

angle to drain. Especially when tiny seeds are involved, watering with a can from above is bad practice as it can 'puddle' the surface of the compost and cause it to lie wet.

If a sheet of glass is then placed over the pot or tray, further watering should not be needed until the seeds have germinated. The glass should be slightly larger than the container so that it rests on the edges. If the surface does dry out, it is possible to water the same way as before. It is also a good idea, especially with fine seed, to put a sheet of newspaper over the glass to prevent the temperature rising too high and, possibly, delaying germination.

There are too many variables to be able to say how long germination will take but it would normally be between one and two weeks; some seeds can take less time while some may take considerably longer. Once there are signs of germination, the paper and glass can be removed and the seedlings allowed to grow on their own.

Filling up a tray of small pots prior to insertion of seedlings.

Lifting a few seedlings at a time from their existing seedtray.

Striking off the surface of the compost to give an equal amount of compost in each 'pot'.

Making a hole in the compost to receive the roots of the seedling.

Gently firming the compost.

When sowing fully hardy plants, such as most vegetables, it is normally better to sow them either directly where they are to grow outdoors or in seed trays that are kept outdoors. The higher temperatures in a greenhouse may delay or even prevent germination. The exception to this is when sowing, for example, French or runner beans individually in 3–3.5-in pots in mid-spring for planting outside about a month later, when the risk of a frost is more or less over.

Sowing French bean seeds in the spring to make sure that they germinate quickly. They will later be planted outside when the risk of frosts is over. You can do the same with runner beans.

An individual seedling in its individual 'pot'.

Putting the seedling's roots into the hole in the compost.

Watering in the seedlings.

Gently firming in the roots.

Some specialist seeds, such as the choicer hardy primulas, may even need a period below freezing to trigger the germination process. These should be kept outdoors after sowing in pots.

Although it is normally safer to use bought (packeted) seed, many gardeners also like to use 'saved' seed that has come either from their own garden or from that of a friend. This is perfectly all right and, indeed, half the fun of gardening is derived from acquiring seeds and plants from all and sundry. However, it is normally unwise to put

47

too much faith in the viability of these 'free' seeds for important things such as tomatoes, cucumbers and other greenhouse plants. For planting that really 'matters', it is wiser to use packeted seed from a commercial seedsman. Try some saved seed by all means, but do not rely on it. Peas and beans are an exception to this rule; indeed, many gardeners develop their own strains by keeping seeds from their best plants year after year.

One other very important point about saved seed is that it is a waste of time saving seed from F1 hybrid plants. The seeds from which F1 plants are grown are the result of crossing two specific individuals under controlled conditions so that no 'foreign blood' enters the breeding cycle. If seed is saved from a plant that has been grown from two specific parents (an F1 plant), the next generation will be a complete mixture of all the previous generations that went into producing the F1 hybrid.

A date relating to their viability will be found on every packet of bought seed and, even if it sometimes seems to have a very short viable life, it is as well to be guided by this information. However, if there are any seeds left over from a packet, and they are especially desirable or expensive, it may be possible to use them the following year if the packet is closed tightly again and kept in the bottom of a fridge.

VEGETATIVE PROPAGATION

Vegetative (asexual) propagation involves removing part of the plant that is to be propagated and inducing that part to produce roots and, ultimately, grow into a new plant. There is one important benefit to this: while a batch of seedling plants may exhibit very small differences to from their parent, those propagated vegetatively will be identical to the 'parent' plant from which they came. The main advantage of vegetative propagation is that it will produce an infinite number of identical plantlets, and this is the reason why it is used more than any other method in professional plant propagation.

There is another significant benefit in that, when a batch of cuttings from one plant are taken, they should all root within a very short period. This is a great advantage when propagating plants for a living. The vast majority of ornamental greenhouse plants, such as chrysanthemums, carnations and house plants grown for their decorative foliage, are propagated vegetatively.

Tip Cuttings

The most common way of propagating plants vegetatively is from what are called 'cuttings', a rather loose term that can refer to any one of half a dozen things. In simple terms, a cutting is a piece of a plant that is used for vegetative propagation. The actual part used will vary from plant to plant and, in many cases, an individual plant can be propagated vegatatively in a number of ways. The best method will be the quickest, easiest and most productive, and the one that results in the best-looking (well-shaped) offspring. Thus, the part of a plant that is most likely to be used is a section of shoot, usually the one that includes the tip (growing point). This is one of the most active parts of a plant and, since it already has a growing point, it is more likely to produce a good looking 'child' more quickly. This particular type of cutting is called a 'tip cutting' because it involves the tip of a growing shoot.

Pot-grown fuchsias need to be kept under control and tidy by regular pruning. After drying off the plants once they have stopped growing in the autumn, all the dried-up shoots are cut back to a few inches. After this the plants are kept dry and dormant until the spring.

Taking tip cuttings is a good way of propagating fuchsias. Once an existing potted fuchsia has been cut back in the spring and is growing again, with a number of 5–8cm (2–3in) new shoots, it can be used for propagation. In fact, many professional fuchsia growers will take even smaller cuttings – 1cm (half an inch) is not uncommon, and some will even go down to the growing point with just one pair of leaves.

This demonstrates a very important principle in propagating by tip cuttings. The smaller the cutting, the more quickly it will form roots; however, it is also more likely to die if it is not constantly looked after. Cuttings of this size need to be kept in the plant equivalent of 'intensive care'. They may start forming roots in just a day or two, if they can be kept alive that long, but they will need mist propagation and a lot of care. In most cases, it is wise to stick to larger cuttings. They are much easier to root under 'normal' conditions and they represent the main way by which an enormous number of different kinds of plant, both outdoor and greenhouse, are propagated.

Stem Cuttings

Using the same soft shoots, but snipping off about the top 2–3cm (1in) (the growing point), results in a 'stem cutting'. The bottom end should be trimmed immediately below either a single leaf or pair of leaves or a leaf scar. Similarly, the top cut is made immediately above a leaf. This kind of cutting is common in the spring and early summer when there is a lot of new growth, much of which can be used for making cuttings.

The main reason for having a leaf or leaf scar at the base of the cutting is that there is a greater concentration there of the

Filling a half-pot with sowing or multi-purpose compost prior to inserting cuttings.

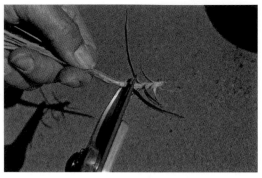

Preparing to take cuttings of laced pinks (or border carnations).

Lightly firming the compost.

Inserting and firming a cutting. Rooting powder and mist propagation will speed up the process.

hormone that induces healing and rooting. Some species will root adequately when the base is between two leaves but these are in the minority. They are called 'internodal' cuttings; the node is the part of the stem where there is a leaf.

Some plants, such as the tender or half-hardy Dracaena and Cordyline, can be propagated when they get tall and 'leggy' by 3- to 5-cm (1- to 2-in) cuttings of the leaf-less section of stem. The cuttings are pushed into a seed and cuttings or multipurpose

Watering the filled pot.

Making a hole with a dibber for the cutting.

Plants with the same trailing habit as ivy can be rooted very economically by laying the stems on the compost and gently pushing the whole length into it, so that much of it is buried. This is called 'serpentine' layering.

The pot full of cuttings.

Woody cuttings usually benefit from dipping the base in hormone rooting powder before insertion.

compost so that the tops are just showing, and placed in greenhouse conditions. After some weeks, roots will form on the base of each section, followed by a shoot from the top. If the cutting is longer than indicated, roots will form throughout its length.

A slightly different method may be used to propagate Ficus, especially *Ficus elastica*, the Rubber plant. Again, the stem is cut into sections, this time ensuring that each one still has a leaf attached to it. It is from the axillary bud where the leaf stalk joins the stem that the new plant arises.

Both these and the leafless stem cuttings are called 'leaf-bud cuttings'. Those with the leaf left on are often called 'mallet cuttings'.

Layering

Ficus is also commonly propagated by 'air layering', normally when the plant has become leggy, top-heavy and unattractive. On the bare section of stem, about 15cm (6in) below the bottom leaf, an upward cut is made so that it goes no more than halfway through the stem. The stem is bent gently so that the cut opens and this is then packed with damp sphagnum moss, or peat fibre. The whole area is wrapped with polythene and secured by sealing the top and bottom of the 'sausage' with sticky tape. During the rest of the growing season, roots will form on the cut stem and will grow into the fibre.

As long as the operation is carried out in the spring, enough root should have developed by the second half of the summer to remove the polythene wrapping, cut the stem below where the roots have formed and pot up the former 'top' of the plant.

If a single-stemmed plant is used, air layering is more of a cosmetic operation to improve the look of the plant; there is no actual increase in the number of plants but it does result in a better-looking one. However, where there is more than one stem – for example, with a multi-stemmed Ficus – each of the stems can be turned into a new plant.

Ordinary 'layering', as opposed to 'air layering', is often used to propagate trailing or climbing plants such as Hedera (ivy), Cissus and Rhoicissus. In natural conditions, these plants nearly always send out adventitious roots from the stems, either to support themselves better or to increase their number. The glory of propagating these is the ease with which a large number of progeny can be grown from a single stem. Also, it is simple. Stems may be either left attached to the parent plant or cut from it and are then laid flat on the surface of a seed tray of compost. Roots will form at the leaf nodes. The method is most successful when the stem is held in position on the compost either by little wire hoops or small stones.

In 'serpentine layering', lengths of, say, ivy stems just shorter than the length of the seed tray are laid on the surface of the compost. The stones or wire hoops are sited between the buds so that, hopefully, the internodes send roots into the compost and the buds grow out into shoots.

Leaf Cuttings

Some plant species, such as Begonia, Saintpaulia and Streptocarpus, have fleshier leaves than most others and the sap within them allows a mature leaf to stay alive for a considerable time, even when parted from the plant. This has led to the mature leaves being used extensively for propagation purposes. Indeed, it is the way in which these plants are normally propagated. Some Peperomias also exhibit this talent, notably *Peperomia*

There are several species of Peperomia well worth growing, notably *Peperomia caperata* and the taller and more vigorous *P. magnoliaefolia*, of which there is a variegated form, but *P. argyreia* (formerly *P. sandersii*) (l) is particularly pleasing with its almost succulent, waxy leaves and comparatively stocky growth. Regular potting on will keep it shapely and growing until, once it is relatively large, it makes a good specimen plant on its own.

argyreia (formerly *P. sandersii*). With Saintpaulias and *Peperomia argyreia*, it is normal to use a whole leaf with a short length of stem retained and pushed just below the surface of the compost. A cluster of new plants will develop from the cut end of the stem.

Streptocarpus differs in that, because the leaves are long and largely strap-shaped, they are cut into sections, each about 5cm (2in) long. The sections are stood upright and the lower end is pushed into the compost. Similar to Saintpaulia, new plants form on the buried end of the midrib.

Because the leaves of *Begonia rex* are so large, there are two different methods. In the first, the leaf is cut up into pieces about 4cm (1.5in) square, so that there is a main vein in every piece. These are inserted into the compost, upright, so that the lower end of the main vein is below the surface. It is from this point that the new growth arises. In the other method, a whole middle-aged leaf is laid on the compost, upper surface upmost, and cuts are made through several of the main veins. These cuts are then pressed into the compost and held there either with wire loops or small stones. As before, new plants form where the veins have been cut.

Although these examples may seem almost miraculous, they are really simply an extension of what happens naturally with cacti and succulents: almost every piece that drops off a plant will form roots and, ultimately, a new plant. There should be no problems, as long as the leaf material is not allowed to dry out and die. This is quite easily done either with a mist unit or a propagator with a transparent lid.

With *Sansevieria trifasciata*, the Snake plant, the leaves can be cut into sections, which are then pushed into the compost, where roots and small plants will develop on the buried part. However, that only applies to those plants that are wholly green. If the leaf has a yellow stripe down the edges, this is *Sansevieria trifasciata laurentii* ('Mother-in-law's tongue') and the whole plant has to be divided. When propagated by leaf cuttings, the resulting plants lose the yellow edge and are all green.

Root Cuttings

Plants that have adventitious buds on the roots are best propagated by root cuttings. These are more or less the same as stem cuttings in that a length of root, with the buds clearly visible, is cut from the plant and divided up into lengths of about 5cm (2in). These are normally laid on compost and then buried under more compost. New plants develop from the buds on the root.

Oddly, there are virtually no tender (greenhouse) plants that are propagated by

Maranta leuconeura **is commonly known as 'Rabbit Tracks', after the pattern of brown 'footmarks' on it's leaves, or 'The Prayer Plant', because it's leaves fold together at night like praying hands.**

Saintpaulia ionantha (I and S), the African violet, is one of the most popular and best-known house plants. However, it is also one of the most challenging to grow well, especially indoors. For a start, they are usually kept in too cold surroundings and this leads to a lack of growth and a lot of old and unattractive leaves. The leaves are covered with fine hairs, which attract dust, and they are also easily discoloured by careless watering. This can be serious if the plant is in a sunny position. The plant is also subject to more than its fair share of pests; notably the tarsonemid mite, a relation to the glasshouse red spider mite. For the gardener who is up to the challenge, *Saintpaulia* is found in a wide range of colours and leaf forms and they look particularly pleasing as a collection.

root cuttings but a good example of a hardy plant is the raspberry. Couchgrass and bindweed also come into this category.

Division

One of the most common, easiest and most successful methods of propagation is division. More or less any plant that is made up of clusters or clumps of shoots from ground level can be divided. Maranta, the Prayer Plant, is a good example. The Peperomias is another group and many ferns also divide well. Saintpaulia (African violet) can be either divided or propagated from leaf cuttings. Strelitzia (Bird of paradise flower) is almost always divided. Seed is the other way but the resulting plant takes many years to reach flowering size.

Division is extremely simple to carry out. In its most rudimentary form, it simply involves taking the plant to be divided out of its container, or digging it up if it is in the greenhouse border, and pulling it apart into two or more new and smaller plants. The main skill lies in breaking up the parent plant into naturally occurring sections. Retaining the pieces from the outside of the original plant ensures that the new plants are young and vigorous. The old centre of the plant should be discarded. The new plantlets are then either planted directly into the border or potted up and grown on, if they are to remain in the pots. After all that fairly brutal treatment they must be looked after well for some weeks, with regular watering and feeding.

The most important part of division is to choose the raw material wisely and with care. Weak divisions will seldom grow into strong plants whereas strong plants with several possible divisions will hardly know that they have had anything done to them.

Plantlets

On a par with division in terms of simplicity comes the last commonly used method of vegetative propagation: the use of plantlets. The universally known *Chlorophytum elatum*, or Spider plant, is the classic example of this method of 'tip layering'. Although large plants of *Chlorophytum elatum* can be increased by division, it is well known for producing its own plantlets on the end of arching stems – the perfect plant for children seeking hands-on experience.

Saxifraga sarmentosa tricolor (Mother-of-thousands) is another example of a plant that produces plantlets.

With all such plants, the way to propagate them is to place smaller pots, filled with compost, close to the parent plant and simply peg the plantlets, still attached to the main plant, into the compost in the smaller pots. Once the plantlet has produced roots that are growing into the compost, and has become a self-supporting young plant, the 'umbilical cord' can be cut.

ROOTING MEDIA, ETC.

In vegetative propagation, the mechanics of the job are remarkably similar, whatever method is being used. Air layering is the odd one out in that the rooting medium, the material in which the new roots are formed, is sphagnum moss or peat fibre. In all other cases, it is usually a 50/50 mix of peat (or substitute) and coarse grit. The peat holds the moisture while the grit keeps the compost open and free-draining. An alternative to grit is an extremely light material called vermiculite, which is super-heated mica that has expanded. (It was at one time used for loft insulation but its structure was found to be too dusty for this purpose.)

During the rooting stage, the rooting medium is simply there to support the cutting and provide something for new roots to grow into. Once rooting has begun, the rooted cuttings are potted up into a potting or universal compost where the fertilizer content ensures that the young plant is healthy.

Various other aids to rooting include hormone rooting powder. Other formulations are available, such as a gel or a liquid into which the base of the cutting is dipped, but there is no substantial difference in their efficacy. One point worth remembering is that the hormone content of all these formulations is fairly short-lived and it is worth buying a new lot every year to avoid disappointment.

Not all plants respond favourably to being treated with rooting hormone; in fact, zonal pelargoniums can be damaged by it. Fortunately, they root pretty readily without it.

EQUIPMENT

There are two plant propagation items of equipment that stand out above all others: an electric propagator and a mist propagation unit.

The electric propagator is particularly useful as it allows a gardener to propagate most kinds of cuttings with a minimum of fuss. In essence, it is simply a large seed tray with warming cables fitted below the base and with a transparent, removable top. It is available in many different sizes.

The cuttings are prepared, pushed into a couple of inches of rooting medium (for example, peat and grit), and given a good watering. The heating cables are switched on and the lid is replaced. After about a week, the cuttings can be given a gentle tweak to see if there are signs of rooting. If there are none, the top is put back for another week before trying again. Once the cuttings have roots 1–2cm (a bit less than an inch) long, they are ready for potting up in a potting compost.

Many variations on the general theme are available, including propagators without heating cables. Most garden shops or centres stock a wide range of sizes and prices.

4   When and What to Grow

WHAT TO GROW

Finally, after all the preparation, it is possible to consider what plants to grow. In the outdoor world, much of the responsibility for success (or otherwise) is down to the vagaries of the prevailing conditions and the weather. Under glass, it is much more down to the gardener, and this is why the planning stages are so important. Some automatic systems can control ventilation and watering, for example, but even these rely on someone to set them up and keep an eye on them.

When it comes to choosing what to grow, much will depend on the type of greenhouse that is involved: it will need to contain the right equipment, be situated in a suitable position and be capable of housing and growing what the gardener wants. Certain groups of plants will benefit from time in the greenhouse, and the first new skill that beginners to greenhouse gardening will learn is probably propagation. This is the raising of plants that will either be planted outdoors at a suitable time, if hardy, or kept in the greenhouse if not. These include many half-hardy annual bedding plants, such as Salvia, Nemesia and Lobelia, along with the hundred and one other 'cheap and cheerful' ornamental annuals and biennials that can be found in any seed catalogue.

Hardy annual, biennial and perennial flowers are best sown directly outdoors as greenhouse conditions are not necessary or even desirable for them.

Another group of plants that will benefit from the greenhouse are certain half-hardy vegetables, such as French and runner beans, cucurbits (marrows, courgettes, cucumbers, pumpkins, and so on) and sweetcorn. Even hardy vegetables, such as summer cauliflowers and broccoli/calabrese, will appreciate a warmer start under glass before being planted outside in late spring, when the outside temperature has, hopefully, risen to a suitable level for steady growth without any cold-weather interruptions. In fact, summer cauliflowers are one of the most difficult vegetables to grow well completely outdoors and anything that can be done to ensure steady growth will be beneficial.

Early peas, although perfectly hardy, can be raised in boxes in the greenhouse before planting outside when they are about 15cm (6in) tall. This will give them a flying start in life and will lead to cropping up to a month sooner than a crop grown outdoors throughout.

The most significant advantage of having a greenhouse, where vegetables are concerned, is the ability to extend the choice to include half-hardy summer vegetables, such as tomatoes, cucumbers, peppers and aubergines, along with winter crops of lettuce, radish, and so on. All of these grow very well under glass, whether heated or not.

With regard to seed-raised fruits, it is possible to grow really choice varieties of melon (such as the cantaloupes) in a heated greenhouse; especially if they are started early in the growing season. Out-of-season strawberries are another favourite and even pineapples are 'growable' in a suitably managed greenhouse, as are virtually all the desirable citrus fruits. The only real difficulty is deciding which to grow because there are so many to choose from

It would be wise to stop short of bananas, mainly because of the size of the plants. If space is not a problem, the most suitable variety would be *Musa acuminata* (formerly *M. cavendishii*), although even this quite easily reaches 3m (10ft) in height, and would leave little room to grow anything else in a modestly sized greenhouse.

SEASONAL CALENDAR

January

Maintain a minimum night temperature of 4–7°C (40–45°F) and try to keep a day temperature of 10–13°C (50–55°F).

Water cautiously and sparingly, only giving most plants enough to prevent wilting.

Hippeastrums (Amaryllis) for spring flowering can be re-potted and started into growth.

Most dormant greenhouse climbers, whether potted or in the ground, will be dormant now and can be pruned, if necessary.

Potted flowering bulbs can be brought inside now for spring flowering.

Buy any pots, trays, composts, liquid feeds and other fertilizers, and so on, in good time for use in the spring.

Sininngia (Gloxinia), tuberous-rooted Begonia and Achimenes tubers can be potted up and started into growth, assuming the the greenhouse is kept warm enough.

Keep the greenhouse spotlessly clean. Always clear up fallen leaves and debris to prevent disease and, once a plant is clearly dead, try to find the cause in order to prevent further cases.

From mid-month, begonias, Cyclamen, Sininngia and Streptocarpus may be sown, but do not be afraid to delay. With the exception of Cyclamen, which has relatively large seeds, the others have almost dust-like seeds and, once sown, these are best put in a propagator where the extra warmth and humidity will help them to germinate.

Start rooting cuttings of early-flowering chrysanthemums.

February

Aim for the same temperatures as for January.

Watering can be more frequent on sunny days; as can ventilating.

Pot-grown fuchsias, and other woody greenhouse perennials, can still be pruned back and started into growth. If any need re-potting, this can be done late in the month using JIP2 compost. Once they have made sufficient growth, these and others, such as Heliotrope and Aloysia (Lippia or Lemon-scented verbena), can be propagated now by softwood cuttings.

Many autumn-potted bulbs can be brought in for gentle forcing.

Seed sowing of summer-flowering greenhouse annuals can begin but the temperature must average 13–18°C (55–65°F) or they will not survive.

These, and many other pot plants, such as ferns and pelargoniums, will start growing before the end of the month and may be potted on (moved into larger pots), if required.

March

Minimum night temperature of 7–10°C (45–50°F) and day temperature of 13–16°C (55–61°F). This higher temperature is necessary because life in the greenhouse is starting again in earnest and the tender young growths need the extra warmth.

More ventilation will be needed on sunny days and also, if appropriate, shading, although not of the more semi-permanent kind, such as whitewash.

Under these conditions, overhead spraying with water may also be needed; avoid spraying open flowers when it is sunny as it can scorch them.

Sowing seeds and taking softwood cuttings can both be continued.

Pricking out seedlings and potting up rooted cuttings must also be attended to. If they are left, they will soon spoil and the roots will become tangled.

Re-pot any orchids that are starting to grow and need it, as well as any pot plants, to avoid them spoiling.

Any vegetable seedlings, such as French and runner beans, marrows, courgettes, and so on, that have been sown under glass for planting outside later on must be grown cool throughout to prepare them for the great outdoors. Many can be put into a cold frame this month when they are large enough.

Keep a sharp eye out for pests and diseases and take action where necessary. Neglect will often lead to worse problems later on. First, identify the problem – without this, there is little hope of a solution – then use the recommended method for eradication, whether chemical or cultural.

Many plants that are normally propagated vegetatively (from cuttings and so on) can be increased now.

Fuchsias, Heliotrope, Coleus and perpetual-flowering carnations can all have cuttings taken, which will root readily in a propagator or under mist. Most of these can also be multiplied by seed but cuttings must be used in order to increase a particular plant.

Many greenhouse plants that were propagated earlier will need potting up or moving into larger pots. Do this before the roots become pot-bound or the plants' growth will be checked.

When potting on Sininngia (Gloxinia) and tuberous-rooted begonias, only half-bury the tubers; keep the base of the stems out of the compost.

April

Keeping the temperatures at March levels is fine, but be aware that they will rise quickly on a sunny morning. Shading, of one sort or another, should be put on this month, and for the rest of the growing season.

Overhead damping will be a regular task on a warm day.

Bulbs that have flowered should be moved outside and encouraged to keep growing to make a good size for next year.

All plants should be regularly fed, preferably with a liquid feed, to ensure steady growth.

Bulbs such as Lachenalia and Ixia that require baking in the summer are best put on their side in full sun to keep them bone dry.

Any seedlings large enough to be pricked out or potted up should be dealt with as soon as they need it.

Nearly all greenhouse plants can be propagated from cuttings at this time of year.

Pot-grown azaleas and camellias will benefit from potting on after flowering. Only those that clearly do not need it, looking at their own size and that of their pot, should be left alone.

May

The outside temperatures prevailing this month are much the same as in April but the days are longer and, therefore, the temperature has more chance of rising too much. The greenhouse floor will need damping down more often on sunny days and more attention will need to be paid to ventilation and shading. This is where automatic vent openers really come into their own.

Any plants that will later be stood or planted outdoors should be put moved as soon as they are large enough so that their space in the greenhouse is made available for the next batch of seedlings and for greenhouse plants that are getting bigger all the time.

The popular winter-flowering primulas P. obconica, P. malacoides, P. sinensis and P. × kewensis should be sown now, along with Senecio (Cineraria), which will also flower next winter.

Varieties of the winter-flowering Erica carnea can be propagated from softwood cuttings either in a propagator or under mist.

Any seedlings of half-hardy or tender annuals that have been raised under glass as flowering pot plants can go into their final pots now. Using 12-cm (5-in) pots will make a really good show. If the plants are still on the small side, two planted together in one pot will soon fill it.

Tuberous-rooted begonias, Sininngia (Gloxinia) and Streptocarpus can go into their final pots when they have outgrown their present ones.

June

From this month onwards, there should be little need to heat the greenhouse, so this is good time to have a look at the heating systems and overhaul or replace them.

Give plenty of air and shade the greenhouse and frames whenever this is needed. With the exception of some 'stove' plants, the rest will be perfectly happy without any heating at this time of year.

Watering will normally be needed twice a day when it is hot. Damping down will often be needed, both on the internal paths and over the plants.

Any half-hardy shrubs can be stood outside with little risk of them coming to any harm, although they should be protected in case of a thunderstorm or hail.

Pests and diseases can be a real nuisance if insufficient attention is paid to keeping on top of them. The most effective way is to fumigate with a suitable smoke, which will penetrate into every nook and cranny, seeking out the enemy. If this is done about fortnightly, or even monthly, the 'baddies' will stand little chance of getting the upper hand.

Hot, dry conditions greatly increase the risk of red spider mite, which can be a big problem with cucumbers, and tomatoes to a lesser extent, under glass. They will be discouraged if the atmosphere is kept damp all the time by regular and thorough damping down.

If you are growing pot cyclamens for winter flowering, they can live outside, preferably in a cold frame, throughout the summer and early autumn.

Polyanthus and primrose seed can be sown in pots for late winter and early spring flowering.

July

Normally the weather in July will be much the same as in June and the main task will be to prevent the greenhouse getting too hot and dry. Not only is this bad for many of the plants but it also encourages certain pests, notably red spider mite. Keep damping down, and consider introducing the parasitic mite *Phytoseiulus persimilis*, which is very effective at keeping on top of red spider. Of course, once the spider has been eradicated, the parasite will starve until the red spider population recovers.

Pinch back winter-flowering chrysanthemums for the last time.

A final sowing can be made now of *Primula obconica, P. malacoides, P. sinensis* and *P. × kewensis* as well as Senecio (Cineraria). This will give successional flowering in the autumn.

East Lothian stocks and mignonette, for flowers and scent the following year, can be sown towards the end of the month for growing in pots.

Hydrangea cuttings, also for growing in pots, can be taken now.

Freesias should be potted for early flowering in the new year. Keep them in a cold frame.

Nerines will be growing well and will need more water.

August

Very similar to July as regards weather, except that the days will be shortening.

Schizanthus, Nemesia and Clarkia can be sown now together with intermediate stocks and cyclamens.

Many bulbs can be planted in pots now, including Lachenalia, Roman hyacinth, early tulips and Narcissi for advancing, as well as polyanthus grown from seed.

Iris reticulata and *I. danfordiae* for pot cultivation can also go in.

Re-pot cyclamen corms that have been rested, along with *Amaryllis belladonna*.

September

The heating will need to be turned on again this month to keep the temperature not lower than about 7°C (44°F).

Chrysanthemums and any potted, woody plants that were moved outside for the summer should come under cover again now.

Any more annuals for winter flowering should be sown early in the month.

Bulbs and annuals that are being grown for winter flowers should be in their final pots now and must be moved from the cold frames on to the shelving in the greenhouse so that they get plenty of light.

Arum lilies that were planted outside for the summer should be lifted, potted up and brought in under cover at the end of the month.

Any other bulbs that are wanted for flowering early in the spring should be bought and potted up as soon as possible.

October

The temperature can be allowed to drop a bit now but should be no lower than 4–7°C (40–45°F).

Over-watering plants at this time of year can kill them.

Any shading should come off.

Plants that are going to over-winter in the greenhouse in one form or another should be suitably hardened off to survive the lower temperature.

Ventilation should be limited to 2 to 3 hours either side of noon so that the temperature in the greenhouse does not drop too low.

Do not neglect to feed perennial plants that will be flowering during the next few months, but go easy on the nitrogen or too much new growth will result. For this reason, a tomato feed (which is high in potash) is perfect for the job.

Tuberous-rooted begonias and Sinningia should be gradually dried off so that they stop growing. Once they are fully dormant, they can be knocked from their pots, dried off completely, cleaned up and stored cold but frost-free until the spring.

Any late-flowering chrysanthemums that are still outdoors must be brought in before the frosts. Feed them with a high-potash liquid feed once a week.

Other plants that will be flowering during the winter can be fed weekly but make sure that these feeds are high in potash, and not nitrogen, as this will encourage flowering as opposed to growth.

Overhaul all heating equipment in readiness for its imminent use. If it is oil-fired, buy in adequate stocks.

Most greenhouse shrubs that have finished flowering can be pruned now. The simplest system, in line with maintaining a good shape, is to shorten back to 5cm (2in) the shoots that have finished flowering.

Many spring-flowering bulbs can still be planted early in the month for forcing. These include hyacinths and late-flowering tulips and Narcissi. After potting, plunge them in used potting compost, or something similar, in a cold frame until growth is progressing nicely.

In the second half of the month, stop watering cacti and succulents until early spring (March). This may sound harsh treatment but it encourages flowering better than anything else and it does not hurt the plants one bit. In fact, it does them a great deal more good than over-watering them. They are using virtually no water through the winter and, under these conditions, wet roots spell death to them.

November

As in October, the temperature should be kept to no lower than 4–7°C (40–45°F).

Ventilation should be necessary only when the sun is actually shining.

All shading can be removed, to allow in the warmth and light of any sunshine.

There should still be some colour in the greenhouse. Begonia 'Gloire de Lorraine' (the winter-flowering begonia) is especially good in a hanging basket. *Primula* × *kewensis*, Boronia and Saintpaulia are also all good and relatively easily grown.

December

Maintain November's temperatures and during this, the darkest month of the year, keep the glass clean to allow in what little light there is. This is also the month when supplementary lighting is at its most valuable, where appropriate.

Watering should be carried out carefully so that the crown of most plants stays dry, greatly reducing the risk of rot. An irrigation or sand bench is especially useful here because the water comes from below the plants and does not wet the top.

Be ready to ventilate a little in all but the coldest weather, to keep the air buoyant and moving.

Make sure that the greenhouse is airtight so that heat cannot escape.

When chrysanthemum plants have finished flowering, cut them down and store them in a cold frame or in a cool corner of the greenhouse. Do not forget about them!

Some hardy flowering shrubs, such as Forsythia and Deutzia, can be cut and brought into the greenhouse for standing in water and bringing into flower.

Greenhouse primulas, such as *P. malacoides*, *P. obconica* and *P. sinensis*, will be coming into flower along with Cyclamen, some chrysanthemums, freesias and Poinsettia.

5 Ornamentals for the Greenhouse

This section lists some of the more common and interesting greenhouse plants that it will be possible to grow, and indicates at what temperature they prefer to be grown. Clearly, there is a fair degree of latitude in this but it gives an idea of which plants can be grown at the three generally accepted temperature ranges: cool house, intermediate and stove house.

COOL HOUSE

Winter: 7–15°C, 45–60°F

Summer: 13–18 degrees centigrade, 55–65 degrees Fahrenheit

The cool house, or the cool section of a large, divided greenhouse, is going to be the busiest, so it should also be the largest in terms of capacity. This is because it will be housing all the young plants that are being raised under glass for planting outdoors when the risk of frost is over. These are, of course, in addition to those that need cool but frost-free conditons throughout their life.

Tibouchina semidecandra (C or I)

This makes a handsome plant that can be grown either in a pot or tub or planted in a greenhouse border. Its vivid purple flowers are produced right through the summer, reaching a peak in the autumn. It is another shrubby plant which, if grown in a container, should have a skeleton of branches

Datura/Brugmansia. The nomenclature, as well as the plants' toxicity, is a minefield; many of the species that have been grown for a long time have changed from *Datura* to *Brugmansia.* Some of the most popular make tall, woody plants, which will soon outgrow a small greenhouse, if allowed to. They are interesting rather than pretty plants and they come in a range of colours, from browny-red, through pale red to yellow and white.

built up over the early years. These are cut back in the spring to allow more flowering shoots to be produced for flowering the same year. It can be kept as small or as large as desired and can be excellent against a wall or up a frame in the greenhouse.

Abutilon

An easy plant to grow and an excellent one for beginners, with no faults or vices in its management. There are both climbers and shrubby species. The most common climber is *Abutilon megapotamicum*, a vigorous plant with dainty red and yellow flowers and the

All parts of *Brugmansia* are poisonous. Another problem is that they are invariably covered in red spider mite, which, of course, will soon spread throughout the greenhouse, if allowed to. Due to its extreme vigour, it is sensible to cut it back hard every spring to leave just stumps. These will quickly shoot again and the skill then lies in keeping only those that are wanted and pulling off the rest when they are a few inches long.

The Abutilon genus (C) is so large and varied that individuals take readily to being grown in many different forms. This results in a variety of plants suitable for growing as shrubby plants, ground huggers and climbers for walls and frames. The shrubby ones are normally cut back reasonably hard in the spring to encourage flowering side shoots to form for the ensuing growing season. Climbing and straggling species, such as A. *megapotamicum*, and its variegated form, are often left to scramble wherever they fancy and are simply cut back, as necessary, in the spring to keep them within bounds.

characteristic protruding centre. There is also a variegated form. One of the best shrubby ones is *A. striatum thompsonii*. It produces 7cm (3in) wide orange flowers in summer but its main attraction is its medium-sized maple-shaped, heavily variegated leaves.

Abutilons like a bright position and plenty of water during the summer, but in winter they go almost dormant and watering should be minimal.

Propagation is by seed sown in early spring or semi-ripe cuttings in late summer or early autumn.

Agapanthus

Although this is a plant that will happily grow outdoors in a frost-free and sunny situation, where this is impossible it can also be grown in pots or tubs, which can be moved outdoors for the summer when all risk of frost is over. Modern plant breeding

Agapanthus (C) is increasingly popular, with many new species and varieties being introduced every year, with differing flower colours and sizes. The most successful way to grow them is to treat them as half-hardies (frost tender) by keeping the pots or tubs in a cool greenhouse during the winter and spring and bringing them outside for the summer, when they are in flower.

has led to a wide choice of species and varieties in the blue, white and lilac range and many new ones are available of different size and vigour. They tend to flower best when almost pot-bound.

Abundant water is needed when growing but they should be dried off completely when winter approaches and over-wintered frost-free and under cover.

Propagation is simply by splitting up the larger plants.

Amaryllis

Botanically, this greenhouse plant is *Hippeastrum hybrida*, but it is usually known as 'Amaryllis'. It is a favourite in midwinter, when its large, trumpet-shaped flowers make a spectacular show; it is available in white and various shades of red, both entire and striped.

After flowering, keep the plant growing to feed the bulb for flowering again the following winter. When the leaves start to turn yellow, stop watering, and dry off the bulb by laying the pot on its side in the greenhouse. When it shows signs of coming to life again in the autumn, watering should restart.

Amaryllis thrives on being pot-bound and re-potting should take place only if the plant has lifted itself out of its pot or has actually split it.

Propagate by pulling the cluster of bulbs apart during dormancy and re-potting. Alternatively, allow seed to form and sow this when ripe.

Azalea (Including Kurume)

A popular winter-flowering pot plant on the borderline of hardiness, only needing to be kept frost-free. For most of the year, it can

Hippeastrum (C) is the botanic name of one of the most showy plants, popularly called Amaryllis. As long as they are treated appropriately, they are easy to grow and may be brought into flower for many winters. The enormous gaudy flowers are often over 15cm (6in) across. The varying mixtures of bright red and white will dominate their surroundings, so the plants are usually best displayed on their own. They thrive on having limited root space and should only be moved into a larger pot when the clump has split or distorted the existing one, or even lifted itself out. When potting on, use a soil-based potting compost and a new pot only 2.5–5cm (1–2in) wider than the old one. Clumps can be split up but this should be done only for multiplication purposes, not for the benefit of the plant.

Hanging baskets are always a good way of taking plants into the third dimension. This unusual choice for growing in a hanging basket is *Begonia × hiemalis* 'Gloire de Lorraine' (C). One of only a few winter-flowering begonias, it came about as a result of crossing *B. socotrana* with *B. × tuberhybrida*.

Begonia

Begonias fall into two broad groups. The majority are 'fibrous-rooted' although the large-flowered show ones are usually tuber-forming plants that are dried off after flowering until the following spring. These succeed best in a frost-free greenhouse. Many of those with a fibrous root system are grown for outdoor bedding plants, but raised under protection.

There are also many specie begonias, some of the most showy of which are the 'cane-stemmed' ones, which can be up to 1.25m (4ft) tall. There are also winter-flowering begonias, such as *Begonia* × 'Gloire de Lorraine'.

Begonia rex is something of a mixture. It is ultimately a large plant with a fibrous root system. It is grown for its richly decorative and large, multi-coloured leaves.

be kept outdoors in a sheltered position, and brought in to the greenhouse only in the autumn for flowering.

Bougainvillea glabra (C) is possibly the king of the climbers and, in the right climate, it can cover a house in just a few years. Unfortunately, this vigour is the very factor that makes it an awkward plant to grow, other than as a pot plant, in a domestic-sized greenhouse. A good system is to allow it to become established in the first couple of years by training it so that it develops a good framework of branches in either a flat (two-dimensional) or circular (three-dimensional) form, depending on the amount of room available. Thereafter, every spring, as the first signs of growth are seen, the previous year's flowering shoots are cut hard back to the framework of older branches so that new growths are sent out. These are then tied in as they grow so that the plant is never allowed to become untidy.

The romantic Bougainvillea is definitely for the intermediate house or indoors in the UK. In southern Italy, and elsewhere with a Mediterranean climate, it is a rampant climber as is apparent here.

Prepared hyacinth bulbs. The blue ones have not been plunged outside for long enough before brining them indoors. This leads to shrunken flowers, a common problem for beginners.

Overall, Begonia is a decorative and varied genus.

Bougainvillea

Bougainvillea is often seen covering buildings in Mediterranean countries. In harsher climates, it will grow quite happily in a frost-free greenhouse, either in the ground or in a large pot.

Management is similar to that of fuchsias. Keep the plants almost dry in winter after cutting lightly back in the autumn when flowering has finished. Prune again in the spring when growth starts so that a good shape is formed. Give plenty of light during the growing season.

Propagation is by soft cuttings during the growing season.

Bulbs

No greenhouse is complete without some of the dozens of different and seasonal bulbs that can be grown under cover, in or out of season. They range from daffodils and other species of Narcissus to hyacinths, Hippeastrum, Lachenalia, lilies, tulips, freesias, Nerine and a host of others.

Possibly the most rewarding aspect of bulb cultivation is growing so-called 'prepared' bulbs, mainly of hyacinth. These should be potted in early autumn and left outside in the coolest place possible having plunged their container in, for example, spent potting compost. They are cleaned up and brought into the cool house, or a cold room indoors, in late autumn/early winter and should flower within about a month.

Bulbs flowering in a greenhouse or indoors must be dried off once the flowers are over and the leaves are starting to turn yellow, prior to dying back. Once dormant, the bulbs can, if suitable, be planted outdoors.

'Prepared' bulbs will revert to normal after their first flowering but can still be planted outside.

69

Cacti and Succulents

An enormous group of plants botanically and collectively referred to as 'xerophytes'. The most commonly held fallacy about them is that they must be kept bone dry at the roots. In fact, they thrive under normal, moist soil conditions but there must not be the least risk of waterlogging. If they become wet at the roots, they will die. The main characteristic of xerophytes is that they will *tolerate* dry conditions, but they do not

This belongs to the aptly named genus 'Ferocactus' because of its hooked spines.

This cactus (C) is night-flowering and its long, white, trumpet-shaped flowers are pollinated by moths. When it is almost flowering, a bucket or dustbin, depending on the size of the plant, can be placed over it during the morning and the flowers will be open by the afternoon. Otherwise, it will never be seen in flower, since it is a night-flowering variety.

The winter-flowering succulent *Schlumbergera × buckleyi* (I) is better known as the 'Christmas cactus' in the UK. It is not the easiest plant to grow well, especially when it comes to watering, but is a joy to behold during the dark days of winter. A mixture of organic and inorganic matter (for example, equal parts of peat-based compost and sharp sand) suits it well but, even more important, it must be on the acidic side of neutral. Propagation is in spring by using the leaf sections as cuttings.

A group of superbly grown cacti (C) at a spring flower show.

Another small and pensionable cactus flowering well, as a result of dry winter treatment. Cacti do not *need* drought conditions in the wild or when cultivated, but they can withstand them.

necessarily like them. Some, indeed, such as the so-called 'Christmas cacti', need fairly moist conditions during the growing season if they are to give of their best; however, any hint of waterlogging will kill them.

A solanaceous (potato and tomato family) plant is *Capsicum annuum*, a very close relative of the sweet pepper. It is a very easy annual pot plant to grow and also very colourful. Seed can easily be saved from the brightly coloured fruits but, of course, with such a variable family, there is no guarantee what the progeny will look like.

Calceolaria

The main group of calceolarias that are grown in greenhouses belong to the *C. Herbeohybrida* group, which itself incorporates several species. They are grown mainly as annual pot plants, up to 30cm (12in) tall, from seed sown in summer, which produces flowering plants in the following year. They are easily recognized by their characteristic, balloon-like, spotted flowers.

Capsicum

Many of the more commonly grown species of this very versatile genus, particularly *Capsicum annuum*, are as decorative as pot plants as they are useful in the kitchen.

The size of the fruits varies from a few centimetres long to 15cm (6in) or more. Among the edible ones, the flavour stretches from the mildness of the larger-fruited varieties to the volcanic heat of the small, thin ones. Their colour can be anything from fiery red through orange and yellow, to dark green and almost black.

All are half-hardy annuals and must have frost-free growing conditions, as found in a cool greenhouse. They are best sown in late winter and early spring and kept under cover, at least until the risk of frosts is over. After this, they can be planted in pots or grow-bags and grown in a cool greenhouse or moved outside.

Chlorophytum elatum variegatum

Otherwise known as the 'Spider plant', this is a perfect plant for beginners – quick-growing and easy to look after. A well-established specimen will quickly grow into a large, spreading and drooping adult.

Propagation is also easy. Plantlets are readily produced on the end of side shoots and will quickly form roots when pegged down into pots of compost.

Chrysanthemum

A huge family with species covering most types of plant, from annual bedding plants to the well-known exhibition sprays and singles. The most widely grown by amateurs are the outdoor perennials that are used for cut flowers for the home. Those grown in a cool greenhouse are mainly the ones that flower during the shorter days of autumn and early winter. They may be grown either planted in greenhouse beds or, more often, in large pots.

Countless varieties are available in a wide range of colours, although blues, reds and their derivatives are absent. It is best to buy them as young plants from specialist nurseries in the spring.

As a general rule, greenhouse chrysanthemums need very firm potting so that growth is kept under control. This, in turn, encourages strong and abundant flowering.

The cultivation of chrysanthemums is such an enormous subject that anyone wanting to grow them seriously should consult a book written specifically on the subject.

Cineraria

See Senecio.

Citrus

A very large family of Mediterranean and sub-tropical plants covering the whole range of oranges, lemons, grapefruits, limes and

Oranges and lemons (C and I) are mostly just a bit of fun but Meyer's lemon is the exception as it will produce very usable rather than simply ornamental fruits. They are quite easy to grow; probably the most difficult part of their cultivation is keeping them clear of scale insects. These are easily seen, like tiny tortoises just a couple of millemetres long, on all parts of the plant – leaves, fruits, stems – where they secrete 'honey dew', a sticky sort of sap, on which 'sooty mould' soon develops. Useful oranges are not nearly so easy to grow in the UK as they require much more sun to ripen and sweeten than is usually enjoyed in northern latitudes. An interesting little plant is × *Citrofortunella microcarpa* (formerly *Citrus mitis*). Its fruits are less than an inch across but make up for this by being the sharpest and most acidic thing imaginable. We used to grow this at Writtle and put it near the front of the staging for the benefit of the students!

One of the most peculiar Citrus is the 'Fingered citron' or 'Buddha's hand'. It has no conceivable use and has only its bizarre appearance to commend it. It is a bit of fun though, especially as a pot plant fruiting on the dinner table.

Drejerella guttata (formerly *Beloperone guttata*) (C) has the common name of 'Shrimp plant', in reference to the colour and unusual shape of its inflorescences, which resemble shrimps or prawns. Although it makes a good pot plant, it is at its best when it is grown in the ground and allowed to develop into a shrub. In either situation, regular trimming will keep it compact and full of flowers.

their hybrids. Most of them make excellent cool-house plants and will, under appropriate conditions, fruit quite readily. However, they are not really a worthwhile crop.

Alongside the edible ones, there are those that are solely grown for their ornamental value. One of these is *Citrus mitis*, now more correctly called × *Citrofortunella microcarpa*, which is one of the smallest and hardiest and can stand several degrees of frost. Ultimately, it will make a handsome metre-tall pot plant. Fruits follow the sweetly scented flowers and both can be found throughout the year. The fruits are up to 3cm (just over 1in) across and have the sharpest taste of any citrus fruit.

Mostly, the citrus plants are Mediterranean plants and will grow quite easily in a cool greenhouse. They can be put outdoors in the summer. Fruiting is encouraged by gently brushing across the flowers to disperse the pollen for fertilization.

Citrus meyeri, or Meyer's lemon, is the most successful fruiting lemon.

Seed from bought lemons is quite easy to germinate and grow but the progeny is seldom worthwhile as the whole genus cross-pollinates readily to produce countless hybrids.

Formerly *Coleus blumei*, this handsome and colourful house plant is grown entirely for its colourful foliage, which stands alone for brightness and pure showing off. Officially, it has been renamed *Solenostemon scutellarioides*, but there seems little likelihood of this being adopted by gardeners.

73

Although physiologically a perennial, it is normally treated as an annual, with new plants being raised each spring from seed or, a little later, from soft stem cuttings. Plants kept for longer tend to get leggy unless continually pinched back during the growing season.

Where frosts are rarely, if ever, seen, they can be grown outdoors.

There are many named varieties, but it is usually more interesting simply to sow a packet of seeds and select the best from what comes up.

Cyclamen persicum

This cyclamen makes an excellent winter-flowering pot plant. The key to success with it is to recognize its intense dislike of a high growing temperature – anything over about 15°C (60°F) tends to result in yellowing foliage and general sickliness. They can be grown on from year to year relatively easily. Once flowering has finished, the foliage will start to go yellow and die back. Watering should be stopped when this happens and the plant must be allowed to die back. After 2–3 months' dormancy, new leaves will start to appear and feeding can start again, with weak feeds about fortnightly. If a plant takes a long time to start re-growing, it can be given more water.

Fatsia japonica

Fatsia japonica is one parent of × *Fatshedera lizei* (*see below*), with leaves that resemble those of ivy, although they are up to 30cm (12in) or more across. It makes a handsome pot plant, but it needs plenty of room, because of its size and vigour. Try to mix it with flowering pot plants or it can look a bit gloomy on its own. It really likes being under the staging of the greenhouse where it thrives

in the damp and dim surroundings. In all but the coldest districts it can be planted outdoors, where it will stand quite a lot of frost.

× Fatshedera lizei

This plant gets its generic name from its parents, *Fatsia* and *Hedera* (ivy), and comes somewhere between a shrub and a climber. Young plants are naturally single-stemmed and need supporting. This habit can be changed by removing the growing point when the plant is still quite small so that another bud, lower down the stem, grows out into a side shoot.

A good system with a single-shoot plant is to include it in a group of other and shorter plants, where it will add height.

Propagation is from either terminal cuttings some 7cm (3in) in length or, more economically, from 'mallet' cuttings, in which the top 30cm (12in) or so of the stem is removed and cut into lengths, each with a bud and a leaf.

The variegated form is the most decorative.

Ferns

One of the best places in which to grow ferns is the greenhouse, where they stay in much better condition than outside. Most of them are evergreen, unlike hardy (outdoor) ferns.

As well as the Maidenhair fern, many others can be grown very successfully. Pteris, Nephrolepis, Asplenium and Pellaea are some of the easiest.

Ficus

The Ficus (fig) genus has a huge number of species, many of which are suitable as house plants. The best known is *Ficus elastica* (Rubber plant), with its large, laurel-shaped, shiny, dark green leaves. *F. e.* 'Decora' is the best selection. There is also a very pretty variegated form.

F. benjamina, or Weeping fig, also makes a good house plant, reaching 2m (7ft) tall and with leaves just 6cm (2.5in) long. Here again, there is a variegated form and another with crinkly-edged leaves. The daintier *F. pumila*, or Creeping fig, has a more ivy-like habit.

Freesia

Freesias are gloriously scented, winter-flowering bulbous plants (which grow, strictly speaking, from a corm). A form whose bulbs have been specially prepared can be planted outdoors in spring for summer flowering.

For winter and early spring flowering under cover, the bulbs are planted in succession from late summer to early winter and are kept cool until they have a good showing of leaves. They are then brought into the cool greenhouse, again in succession, where they will stand a little more heat until flowering.

Fuchsias

Fuchsias are some of the most popular plants for a cool greenhouse and also among the easiest and most rewarding. They are almost hardy and are often brought into flower in the cool house before being put outdoors for the summer. They are normally brought under cover for the winter once the tops have been caught by the frost. During late winter, start them into growth again in the cool house.

Propagation is by short, terminal stem cuttings taken as soon as they are available in the spring. Standards are grown on a permanent stem about 60cm (2ft) tall. In other respects, their cultivation is the same as for 'bush' plants.

Geraniums

'Geraniums' is a very broad name for the plants that are grown in a greenhouse. True geraniums are hardy, herbaceous perennials that are grown exclusively outdoors. The half-hardy (greenhouse) ones are either 'Zonal' or 'Regal' pelargoniums. They are cultivated in about the same way as fuchsias in that they are over-wintered either under the greenhouse staging or elsewhere under straw in a frost-free place. In spring, they are normally cut hard back and started into growth again. In this way they make more compact and better plants.

Once the risk of frost is over, the two species take a different course: the Zonals are usually planted outside for bedding, once the risk of frosts is over, and the Regals are grown on in pots and moved either into tubs outside on terraces, for example, or kept in a cool greenhouse as pot plants.

Two other groups, the miniatures and those with scented leaves, are treated more or less the same as Regals.

Grevillea robusta

In its native Australia, this makes a handsome tree, but in cooler countries it is usually grown as a 'dot plant' up to some 90cm (3ft) tall to add height to schemes in large, formal beds. Alternatively, it can be grown as a half-hardy sapling to be part of a display in a cool greenhouse or indoors.

Hedera helix

Common ivy exists in so many shapes, sizes, forms and colours that it is one of the most versatile plants for both outdoors and in a cool greenhouse, adding height and depth to any collection of plants. It is certainly best when the plants are kept for just a couple of years or so as some forms tend to lose their leaves from older wood and the stems become bare and ugly. However, propagation from stem or single leaf-bud cuttings taken early in the growing season is so easy that multiplication is no problem at all. Indeed, when an ivy stem is in contact with the medium on which the plant is standing, it will readily root by itself in just a matter of weeks.

As well as a range of colours, from dark green through mid- and light green to every shade of yellow as well as white, many other species and varieties have leaves in a variety of shapes and sizes.

Ivy is truly a valuable and versatile plant both as a specimen and as a filler and foil in larger displays.

Hibiscus rosa-sinensis

Hibiscus has the great virtue of flowering during the winter. The plant itself is woody and stays reasonably compact but can reach 2.5m (8ft). The flowers are typically bright rose-red with a large, red, protruding stamen but they can also be pink, red or even yellow.

This hibiscus was growing in Italy.

Propagation is by softwood cuttings taken throughout the spring and early summer and rooted in a propagator.

Hydrangea macrophylla

Normally thought of as a hardy garden plant, several hydrangeas can make splendid cool-greenhouse and house plants, including most of the 'lace cap' ones. Usually, they are grown in pots and planted outside in the garden after their first flowering. If kept for greenhouse use after the first year, they tend to get too big and leggy.

They are propagated from softwood cuttings taken in mid-spring.

Jasminum polyanthum

This plant, and its varieties, are some of the best cool-house plants, with a pleasant and all-pervading scent. They are normally grown in pots but, if the greenhouse is large enough, some can be planted in the ground at the base of an upright, where they will clamber upwards with vigour and ease.

Occasionally, they should be rejuvenated by pruning hard back to main shoots after late winter to early spring flowering, encouraging new growth. Some are extremely vigourous and even invasive.

Mandevilla laxa

Still often called *Dipladenia*, this is a tropical climber from Brazil which, although it does appreciate greenhouse protection, is perfectly easy to grow and is almost frost hardy. It is a thoroughly handsome plant with trumpet-shaped flowers of red, pink or white. If it becomes too large and vigourous, it can be cut back hard and it will re-grow readily. It is almost evergreen.

Musa velutina

One of the few banana species that does not need a tropical temperature to grow successfully. In fact, it will tolerate a touch of frost. It should not be grown with any expectation of fruit, but purely as an ornamental plant. If flowers start to appear, they must be pinched out at once; they will never develop fruit and could start a rot, which can spread into the plant.

It will grow to at least 1.5m (5ft) tall, so it really needs a large conservatory or greenhouse.

The smallest Musa species that will produce usable fruit is *Musa acuminata* (formerly *M. cavendishii*); *see* the 'Stove House' section.

Peperomia

Several Peperomias make excellent pot plants, both for the cool greenhouse and indoors. They are grown mainly for their decorative leaves, which come in many shapes and sizes.

Peperomia argyreia (formerly *P. sandersii*) is not always easy to find but it is well worth searching for. Its fleshy, heart-shaped and striped leaves always attract attention. It makes a small plant 15cm (6in) tall.

Another fleshy-leaved one is *P. magnoliaefolia*; its leaves are variegated yellow, light green and darker green. It makes a larger plant than *P. argyreia*.

All varieties prefer a bright situation but not in direct sunshine.

Pericallis cruenta

Better known by its former name of Cineraria and, after many years, still a firm favourite and easily grown in a cool greenhouse. It comes in a wide range of colours, from pale pink to deep blue and purple. It is generally at its best throughout the spring with large plants able to reach 50cm (18in) across. A group of three or four can dominate a room indoors.

Seed is sown in mid-spring for the earliest plants and in the winter for spring flowering.

Good air circulation within the greenhouse or room is essential to prevent *Botrytis* (grey mould) setting in. This means that slatted staging is preferable to sand or gravel in the greenhouse.

Plumbago auriculata

Still known better as *Plumbago capensis*, this is a vigorous scrambler rather than climber, having a similar growth habit to the summer-flowering outdoor jasmines. Although it is normally regarded as a cool-greenhouse subject, pot-grown plants are perfectly happy outdoors during the summer months in the UK. The clusters of lovely sky-blue flowers provide an entirely unexpected colour.

In either case, the best way to train it is to tie it loosely to a support and allow it to have its way. Keep the compost only just moist during its dormant winter period and cut the growths back to semi-permenant woody shoots in the spring to encourage new growth and better flowers.

Saintpaulia ionantha

The very familiar African Violet is popular both as a house plant and for the cool greenhouse. Since the original ones with oval leaves and deep purple flowers appeared during the 1950s, plants have been bred with crumpled leaves, wavy-edged leaves and in colours from every shade of violet, blue, pink and even white.

Supports for climbing plants can easily be made at home using a few split or thin canes. Two canes, one longer than the other, are pushed into the compost on opposite sides of the pot. Another is tied unevenly to the two original canes so that it is slightly sloping. A fourth cane is tied above the third, sloping the opposite way. This sequence can be extended upwards for as far as is necessary. Where older and larger plants are concerned, thicker and longer canes can be used to accommodate the extra growth. The same system can be used three-dimensionally, when even larger plants in larger pots are involved. Making the whole system at home from canes will save pounds in comparison to buying an expensive manufactured frame.

Mandevilla laxa (C or I) (formerly *Dipladenia*) is a spectacular climber with brilliant flowers of dark red, scarlet, pink or white. Some species are almost hardy. It makes a good plant for the cool greenhouse or home, flowering virtually all summer long. It is usually trained on a frame with all the new growth being tucked in. Because of its vigour, it is usually best to enlarge the frame during the first few growing seasons. It should be almost dried off and allowed to rest during the winter. The white sap can be a slight irritant.

One thing to guard against is allowing water to remain on the leaves. Even rainwater, and certainly tap water, will result in a chalky deposit and, if sun shines on the water, it can actually scorch the leaf.

There are now many named varieties covering all the leaf and flower variations but, horticulturally, the original is still the purest, prettiest and most popular. None of the other species and varieties that exist in cultivation is a patch on *S. ionantha*.

Propagation of the 'pure' type is by seed, division and leaf cuttings but the named varieties, can only be increased by vegetative methods.

Salpiglossis

Salpiglossis is a perfectly hardy outdoor annual but it has such an exotic appearance that it is also ideal for adding height to cool-house displays. It is always grown from seed. To flower from mid- to late spring, it is sown under glass in early autumn. To flower from early summer, it is sown in mid- to late winter.

Sansevieria trifasciatae

Sansevieria trifasciatae is better known by the common name of 'Mother-in-law's tongue'. The most popular variety is *S.t.* 'Laurentii', which has a yellow stripe along each edge of the fleshy, sword-like leaves. The 'norm' simply has mottled green leaves.

More than virtually any other plant, with the possible exception of Aspidistra, Sansevieria has the virtue of being able to withstand a degree of neglect that would almost certainly otherwise be fatal.

Propagation of 'Laurentii' should be by division of the clump. Leaf cuttings, which would seem to be the obvious way, give rise to un-variegated plants.

Plumbago auriculata (formerly *P. capensis*) (C) is usually grown in the pale blue form, although there is also a white one. When in full flower throughout the summer, there are few plants more spectacular. No conservatory or cool house should be without it. Like Winter jasmine, it needs support to stop it falling over, so it should be grown against, and tied loosely to, a wall or other support. Potted specimens can spend the summer outside until the autumn frosts. Propagation is normally by soft cuttings in the spring or early summer.

Plumbago auriculata growing in perfect harmony with a pink Campsis. The picture was taken on a Mediterranean island but both plants will grow perfectly well in a cool house in the UK and even outdoors in frost-free areas.

Solanum capsicastrum (Winter Cherry)

The Winter cherry is a long-standing and easily grown favourite for late autumn and winter interest. Although the plants can be saved from year to year, they are so easy to grow that it is simpler to save seed from one of the 'cherries' and sow this 'fresh' in late winter. Choose the seed from the best plant available.

Propagation can also be by cuttings taken in late winter.

Strelitzia reginae

The Bird-of-paradise flower or Crane flower is quite easy to grow but not so easy to bring into flower. The flower stems and leaves can be up to 1m (40in) tall so it is big in every respect. Like most large plants, it is best planted in the ground rather than grown in a pot. However, in a pot, the root restriction does tend to make it flower earlier in its life.

Sunshine is essential for good results and the lack of this is the usual cause of failure. It should be nearly dry at the roots in winter.

Tibouchina semidecandra

This rather lax-growing shrub is a very pleasing and worthwhile plant to grow. With velvety leaves and vivid light purple flowers borne from spring onwards, it may be grown either in a large pot or directly in the cool greenhouse soil. When pot-grown, it may be moved outside during the frost-free season. Slightly acid soil is preferred.

Keep it well watered during growth but almost dry when not. Propagate by semi-ripe cuttings.

Vriesia splendens

The so-called 'Flaming sword' is a popular bromeliad and of a genus having slightly narrower leaves than the broader Aechmea. The leaves are rather pale green crossed with broad brown stripes, and the flowers are vivid flame colour, as the name suggests, and flat.

As with most bromeliads, which live in the wild on the branches of trees, the growing material must be free-draining with a high percentage of sharp sand in fibrous peat and sieved garden compost. It should be easy to grow as long as the temperature is above about 10°C (50°F).

Propagation is from side shoots often produced after flowering.

Zantedeschia

Zantedeschia aethiopica, the Arum lily, has undergone a remarkable change in recent years as regards the range of colours available. In addition to the normal white (rather

Strelitzia reginae (C), the Bird of paradise flower, is far easier to grow than its flamboyant appearance might indicate. It grows perfectly happily outdoors in Madeira and will be fine in a cool house in the UK. The difficulty lies in getting it to flower. Best results are had by growing it in the greenhouse border, rather than in a pot, as it needs the better growing conditions. Unlike many other greenhouse flowering plants, constriction of the root system is not necessarily the key to success.

Cordyline terminalis.

81

Clerodendrum thomsoniae **is a beautiful plant; its pure white flowers with brilliant scarlet are spectacular, but it is not the easiest to grow. It needs warmth all year round, (15–18°C, 60–65°F) and this is usually the stumbling block. Though officially a climber, if the growths are pinched back regularly during the growing season, the plant can be induced to adopt a more bushy habit.**

Sinningia spp. (I), previously known as Gloxinia, adds a touch of the exotic to any greenhouse plant collection and makes an equally good house plants. The colour range is enormous and growing them from seed ensures a wide variation. Like tuberous-rooted begonias, they are truly perennials in that their corm will rest over the winter and then start into growth again each spring. Again, like begonias, they can be propagated from leaf cuttings. Although single plants are pretty, a group of three or more contrasting colours is much more showy.

too funereal for many people), it can now be had in different shades of cream, yellow, pink and pale purple.

Temperatures to below freezing can be tolerated for short spells.

INTERMEDIATE HOUSE

Winter: 13–21°C, 55–70°F
    Summer: 16–24°C, 60–75°F

Achimenes grandiflora

The Hot water plant earned its common name because its generic name, Achimenes, is the Greek for 'suffers from the cold' (which could be said of any number of plants). It does prefer the warmth, and is better in the intermediate house than in the cool house.

The main colours of the flowers are maroon and, less commonly, purple.

It is propagated from the underground rhizomes that develop during each growing season. These are potted up in the spring and covered with fibrous compost to 2cm (about an inch) depth and 1cm (half an inch) apart. It is important when growing Achimenes never to let the compost dry out.

Allamanda cathartica

A. cathartica, or Golden trumpet, needs a warm and humid atmosphere so is essentially a greenhouse plant rather than a house plant. Give plenty of water when growing but keep the compost almost dry during dormancy. It will grow as a climber if encouraged to but can be coaxed, instead, into becoming a small tree, where there is enough room.

Propagate from soft cuttings in spring and early summer. Insert these individually into small pots of equal parts of sharp sand and leaf mould or peat.

Amaranthus caudatus

Commonly known as the 'Tassel flower', this specie is the tender version of the garden flower, also known as 'Love lies bleeding'. It is essentially a tender annual and, as such, is sown under glass in early spring. When large enough, it is moved into either larger pots or the greenhouse border. In the autumn, when it has ceased to be attractive, it is relegated to the compost heap.

Ananas

The genus that covers pineapples and its decorative relatives. Although fruiting pineapples (*A. comosus*) can be grown in a suitably heated greenhouse, it is normally beyond the capabilities of the hobby gardener. Along with *A. bracteatus*, it can be grown into a good plant for the intermediate house, especially the variegated forms. A minimum winter temperature of 13–15°C (55–60°F) is needed. In the summer, it needs to be 16–20°C (60–68°F).

Anthurium scherzerianum

The Flamingo flower is a well-known but seldom grown house plant, or one for the greenhouse where a minimum winter temperature of 16°C (60°F) is possible. It is, by comparison with many other tropical greenhouse plants, relatively small, being some 50cm (20in) tall.

It is grown for its brilliant red spathe (the shield-like hood that surrounds the actual flower). Its large, shield-shaped leaves are shiny, dark velvety green.

Aphelandra squarrosa

The Zebra plant is a well-known sub-tropical plant suitable for either the intermediate greenhouse or for indoors. Its striking green leaves with the herringbone veins picked out in vivid yellow are as well known as the bright yellow spike of the many angular and clustered flowers in the centre of the plant. *A. s.* 'Louisae' is the most widely grown form.

Begonia rex

B. rex is just one member of the enormous Begonia family and one of the most showy, variable and impressive. Although there are many named varieties of Begonia, the dozens of variations shown in *B. rex* are just that: variations. Officially, they are all hybrids under the general heading of 'Rex-cultorum hybrids', of which there are many hundreds.

One specie that originally came in the 'Rex' category is *Begonia masoniana* 'Iron Cross', which is now a recognized specie.

B. rex does require a certain degree of warmth in the winter, with a minimum of 15°C (60°F) required to maintain good health and appearance. A high-potash liquid feed is recommended during the growing season. Those plants with velvety leaves give of their best in slightly shady conditions whereas those with a high degree of red or maroon in their colouring prefer a bright situation.

B. rex is propagated by leaf cuttings. Cutting the leaf into one-inch squares and either laying them flat on the compost or pushing a basal corner with the most main veins into the compost works well. Another way is to select a healthy leaf, cut through the main veins in several places and lay it flat on the compost, vein side down, then hold it in place with small stones.

Once plantlets have formed and have sufficient root, they can be potted up singly. Maintain a temperature of about 20°C (68°F) throughout the propagation and weaning period.

Bougainvillea glabra

This exotic-looking climber is available in several colours, including bright and pale red, orange and almost yellow. It is normally seen growing in an intermediate house, and sometimes even indoors. In its more natural home, it can grow into an enormous climber and is widely seen on the northern shores of the Mediterranean. This might give the impression that it would be impossible to keep within bounds in a greenhouse or indoors, but this is not the case.

Bougainvillea will tolerate a temperature as low as 7°C (45°F). Indeed, this sort of temperature, along with being grown in a pot rather than in the ground, seems to lead to a very much better flowering habit. Grown in a pot, it can also be restricted to 1.5–2.5m (5–8ft).

Propagate, with bottom heat, from soft cuttings taken in late winter/early spring.

Brunfelsia pauciflora (B. calycina)

A pleasing, rather than a 'must-have', plant of about the same shape, size and appearance as Allamanda, with lilac-coloured flowers instead of yellow. The large, shiny, rhododendron-shaped leaves go perfectly with the flowers. It can be grown either in a pot or, even better, planted in the ground. It is on the borderline of hardiness and prefers slightly cramped roots for the best flower power.

Propagate from softwood cuttings taken in spring or summer.

Codiaeum variegatum pictum

Codiaeum vies with Coleus for the most colourful leaves. The main difference is that it will grow into a true, woody perennial and is grown as such. There are also a far greater number of leaf variations, with many named varieties.

It needs a winter temperature of 10–13°C (50–55°F).

Propagation is by air layering or tip cuttings.

The white sap of Codiaeum may cause problems to sensitive skin and should be washed off at once if there is any contact.

Cycas revoluta

An extremely ancient plant, going back to pre-history, and believed to live for up to 500 years. It is very slow-growing, but it makes a handsome and interesting plant for the intermediate house and as a house plant.

A tuft of large, fern-like leaves grows from the base/trunk, which is about the size and shape of a tennis ball. The leaves are some 30cm (12in) and more long, and look rather like ostrich plumes or palm leaves.

Cyclamen persicum

Cyclamen is a large genus that covers all the hardy outdoor plants, as well as those for the house, in all their sizes, colours and different flower shapes. As a house plant, and in an intermediate greenhouse, cyclamens flower mainly, and at their best, in the winter.

Many of the medium-sized ones, and particularly the white-flowered ones, are sweetly scented.

Cycads (l) are ancient plants, with nine species. They are normally grown in pots (front, on the ground). The large specimen in the square tub is a great age. Small, potted plants make an interesting subject of conversation but care should be taken, as they are poisonous. Established specimens will stand a short period below freezing but this is not advisable and intermediate house conditions are recommended.

A great virtue of indoor cyclamens is that, although they are usually treated as annuals, they can quite easily be kept from year to year, given the proper treatment. After flowering, they will grow on for a period, building up their strength for their next flowering. When they stop growing and the leaves begin to yellow, watering should be gradually reduced until it is clear that the corm is completely dormant.

The corm should then be kept cool and dry until it shows signs of growth, when the whole process re-starts, leading to flowering again.

Cyperus alternifolius

Along with the Cycad, this is another plant that can be traced back into the mists of time – *Cyperus papyrus* was used by the Ancient Egyptians for making the very earliest versions of paper.

C. alternifolius is the one normally cultivated. It can stand growing with its rootstock 30cm (12in) under water.

Its requirements for successful growth are fairly simple: most importantly, it needs a winter temperature of no less than 5°C (40°F), and adequate moisture at the roots.

Ferns

The greenhouse is one of the best places in which to grow ferns and there will be appropriate ferns for any of the growing conditions that can be created. Most of them are evergreen, unlike hardy (outdoor) ferns. The only attention that they need is the removal of dead and dying leaves.

Besides the Maidenhair fern, there are many others that can be grown very successfully. *Pteris, Nephrolepis, Asplenium* and *Pellaea* are some of the easiest. Those suitable for the intermediate house include *Adiantum* and some *Nephrolepis*.

Some can be increased by spores but they do not all produce them, especially the more ornate ones. Germinating the spores and growing on the plantlets also demands a certain level of skill. The most reliable way of propagation is by division. The ferns are tipped out of their pot and two hand forks are pushed into the rootball back to back in the centre. The handles are levered together and the rootball will, with a little persuasion, split apart. This should be carried out in late winter, while the plants are still dormant and they will hardly know that anything has happened to them. The new plants will soon start to grow again.

In general, ferns thrive best in shady and humid conditions. The unnatural shedding of fronds is usually a sign that they are subject to too much light. The best place for them is under the staging or amongst other, taller plants. Bearing in mind their preferences, ferns in general do not make very good house plants, although there are exceptions.

The Staghorn fern, *Platycerium bifurcatum*, is hardly recognizable as a fern, with its overlapping 'plates' (the sterile fronds) and antler-like fertile fronds growing out between them. Like most ferns, it likes a moist atmosphere so is better for the cool greenhouse than indoors.

Maranta leuconeura

Sometimes known as the 'Prayer plant', because of its habit of folding its leaves upwards in the evening, or as 'Rabbit's tracks', from the leaf markings. It makes a good house plant but is happier in the damper atmosphere of the intermediate house. There are a number of species and varieties with different leaf colourings.

Propagation is by pulling off 'sections' with two or three leaves from the outside of the plant and rooting them.

Passiflora

Passiflora represents a large genus of vigorous climbers that are interesting rather than beautiful. They produce numerous

Calathea (I or S) is in the same genus as Maranta and there are countless species and variations, all of which are worth growing. As with Maranta, the individual leaves tend to be relatively short-lived but their removal quickly encourages new ones to form. *C. crocata* is the flowering one, *C. zebrina* has the stronger leaf pattern. All three make good house plants but the leaf tips are apt to go brown if the atmosphere is too dry.

flowers in the course of a growing season, but these are spread over a long period, so that there is always a lot of leaf and not much flower. Some species, such as *P. caerulea*, are somewhat more flowerful.

P. edulis, the Granadilla or Passion fruit, produces edible and popular fruits. Others, including *P. caerulea*, have egg-sized orange fruits that are perfectly safe to eat but completely tasteless.

Large plants can be had by maintaining a framework of climbing shoots and branches and just cutting the side shoots hard back in the spring as growth starts. Alternatively, and where space is limited, the whole plant may be cut back to its base as growth starts. Cutting back a plant hard during dormancy does carry the risk of the plant dying.

P. caerulea will survive outdoors on a sheltered, sunny wall. In this case, pruning should be rather less severe.

Peperomia

This genus is large, and diverse in terms of form and appearance. In most cases, the leaves are on stalks that are relatively long in comparison with the size of the plant.

P. argyreia is perhaps the best-looking of the commonly grown species, with particularly nice leaves. They are roundish but with a definite point and with the stalk coming from near the centre of the leaf. The upper surface of the leaf is pale, silvery-green, with the main veins picked out in a much darker green. It makes a bushy plant.

P. magnoliaefolia is a taller plant, again with fleshy leaves, but in shades of green variegated with white. *Ps. caperata* and *scandens* are also good plants that are well worth growing.

All make good house plants.

Poinsettia

The popular winter-flowering pot plant is more correctly *Euphorbia pulcherrima*. A peculiarity is that the brightly coloured red, pink or white 'petals' are actually leafy bracts; the true flowers are yellow and clustered at the base of the bracts. As house plants, poinsettias are normally treated as annuals because they are not particularly easy to keep

The genus Passiflora (C and I), with its many species and varieties, are plants of curiosity rather than beauty. The common name of Passion flower derives from the make-up of the flowers and the number of stamens, which are traditionally believed to represent various aspects of the Crucifixion, including the Crown of Thorns. The one most commonly grown for its ornamental value and ease of cultivation is *Passiflora caerulea*, sometimes called the Blue passion flower, and its varieties. *P. edulis*, the Granadilla, is the only one grown for its edible fruits. (The yellow, egg-shaped fruits of *P. caerulea* are edible without being eatable.) Passiflora plants are vigorous climbers but only a few flowers are carried at any one time, although they do flower over a long period. *P. caerulea* is semi-hardy in the UK – the tops may be killed to the ground in a hard winter but the roots normally survive.

from year to year without a greenhouse. It can be done, however, by gradually drying off the plant after 'flowering' until the leaves and coloured bracts drop off, then shortening the leafless shoots to about 10cm (4in). The plant is kept dry and cool until late spring, when it is watered to start it growing again. It is kept well watered and fed, with any thin and weak shoots being nipped out, to leave about half a dozen.

Then comes the clever stuff. The poinsettia is a 'short-day plant' (as are most chrysanthemums), with flowering being induced by the shortening days of autumn. So, from mid-autumn (late September in the UK) the plant must have fourteen hours of darkness daily. This can be achieved by covering it with, for example, black polythene from early evening until the next morning. Another way is to keep it in an unlit room, as long as the temperature is appropriate. After eight weeks, the plant can be allowed to grow on normally, which should bring it into 'flower' for Christmas.

This timetable, of course, only applies to the northern hemisphere.

Poinsettias need a minimum growing temperature of 13–15°C (55–60°F).

Primulas

Usually thought of as hardy plants, such as primroses, cowslips and polyanthus, the Primula genus also includes a handful of tender ones that are easily grown in a frost-free greenhouse for winter and spring flowering.

Primula obconica has clusters of large flowers, mainly in shades of crimson, blue and pink. (Note: This plant can bring on a rash in some people.) *P. malacoides* comes mainly in reds and purple and with smaller flowers but more clusters. *P. sinensis*

(sometimes called the Chinese primrose) is in reds and pinks, again in 'clusters' on stalks up to 30cm (12in) long, so it is quite a large plant. *P.* × *kewensis*, produces clusters of fragrant, yellow flowers in spring.

All are sown in late spring and early summer and flower from late winter into late spring or even early summer.

Sinningia speciosa (Formerly Gloxinia)

Like many furry-leaved house and greenhouse plants, care has to be taken to keep Sinningia leaves as dry as possible, or *Botrytis* can set in. This is most easily done by watering from below – stand the pots in shallow water until it shows on the surface of the compost. Also, beware of dusty leaves.

Sinningia can be grown from seed sown in mid-spring but it is more usual, and safer, to plant bought-in tubers from late winter onwards. That is also the time to plant tubers saved from the previous year.

Stephanotis floribunda (Formerly S. jasminoides)

This well-known and attractive climber has shiny, dark green leaves and beautifully scented, waxy, white flowers that are carried throughout the summer. Occasionally, one or more of these may be followed by a fruit similar to a small avocado pear. If this is allowed to ripen and split, the seed can be sown in the following spring. Germination is usually excellent.

Stephanotis is better planted in the ground than grown in a pot, although small plants are perfectly acceptable and often more convenient.

Large plants may be controlled by reducing the number and length of the longest and oldest shoots at the first sign of growth starting in the spring.

Streptocarpus

Streptocarpus is gaining in popularity, both as a pot plant for the intermediate house and as a house plant. One nursery, Dibleys, is largely responsible for this and also for the dramatic increase in different shapes, sizes and colours.

Although the plants thrive best in intermediate house surroundings, they will tolerate a cool house as long as they have plenty of indirect sunlight.

Propagation can be by seed but it is so fine as to be dust-like and this method is not recommended for a beginner. Seed should be sprinkled on the sowing compost surface and then covered with a sheet of glass.

Leaf cuttings are much easier. One method is to cut the long and fleshy leaf lengthways along each side of the midrib,

A mixed greenhouse used for both propagation and display, showing how a house can be divided into sections providing different temperature regimes. The near section is the 'intermediate house' and the far section the 'stove'.

which is then discarded. The two resulting strips of leaf are then laid on rooting compost and weighted down with, for example, pebbles, so that the cut edge is in constant contact with the compost. Alternatively, cut the leaf blade crossways into inch-long sections. Stand each section upright and very slightly push it into the compost for stability. The midrib will form roots and a new plant.

STOVE HOUSE

Winter: 16+°C, 60+°F
  Summer: 20–38°C, 70–100°F

Because of the relatively high temperatures required by plants recommended for the stove house, and the resulting cost, the number that can be grown is restricted. In fact, many of the plants often recommended for stove cultivation are perfectly happy in an intermediate house. It is simply that they give of their best when grown in the higher temperature.

Dieffenbachia maculata (D. picta)

The 'Dumb cane', so called because of its toxicity, which will make the tongue swell if it is eaten, is a lovely plant but it does need stove conditions, rather than an intermediate house or a living room, to flourish. It is not an easy plant to grow well, mainly because of the heat and humidity required to keep it happy. The leaf tips are the first things to go brown and, if this happens, care must be taken. Indoors, they are seldom completely at ease, because the conditions that are appreciated by humans are not what they need.

The beautifully coloured leaves at first point upwards but, as they mature, they tend to droop over, making a plant that can reach 90cm (3ft) tall and wide.

Dieffenbachia picta (S), sometimes known as the 'Dumb cane', on account of its bitter sap. As often happens with the most beautiful and desirable plants, *Dieffenbachia* is seriously tropical and needs a minimum growing temperature of 16°C (60°F). Various forms of patterning are found on the leaves and there are named varieties to reflect this. If stove-house conditions can be maintained, *Dieffenbechia picta* is a 'must'.

There are a great many varieties, normally carrying variable amounts of the colours that are present in most of them, that is to say, dark, mid- and pale green with similar shade of yellow.

Propagation is most successful when cutting off and rooting any small, new shoots that appear from the base of the plant. Again, though, adequate heat and humidity are required for them to root and grow.

Gardenia jasminoides

One of the top five greenhouse plants for fragrance, the gardenia is a very difficult plant to grow well, especially indoors. This is mainly because of temperature demands. It needs to be 16–19°C (60–65°F) at night and higher during the day. In addition, it must have plenty of daylight but should not be in full sun. If any of these points is lacking, the flower buds drop off. Conversely, if the flower buds start to fall, then one of these factors is almost certainly to blame.

Altogether a gorgeous plant but one for the specialist; not the average gardener.

Monstera deliciosa

The Swiss cheese plant must be one of the most commonly seen and grown tropical-looking house plant. The large, deeply cut, almost round, dark green leaves can easily measure 45cm (18in) across. These are borne on twisting and turning fleshy stems that will, with maturity, put out fleshy aerial roots. These are most commonly found, along with 'flowers' and fruits, in the stove, where the conditions are much more to the plant's liking than indoors. It is, after all, a jungle plant.

Musa acuminata

Better known under its former name of *M. cavendishii*, this is the smallest species of what can reasonably be called a banana. Its leaves still easily reach 3m (10ft), including the leaf stem, in height, with a similar spread. It therefore needs space as well as stove conditions; without them it is likely to be doomed to failure. In addition, and although a lower temperature is required for vegetative growth, a fruiting plant will need

Monstera deliciosa **(S and I), the Swiss cheese plant, seems to have been around for ever, both in homes and in public places, where it is popular because of its exotic appearance. Its common name reflects the large holes in the leaves. It is an 'aroid' (belonging to the family Araceae) and, coming from the tropics, requires a humid (damp and warm) atmosphere to flourish. Where it grows naturally, its fruits are often eaten as dessert. It is one of the best-looking house plants but not easy to grow well indoors, where the atmosphere is usually warm enough but often too dry.**

27°C (80°F). Given the right conditions in the right greenhouse, though, *M. acuminata* will certainly produce edible fruit.

Plants are sometimes offered for sale at flower shows but, unless they come from a recognized nursery, they are seldom going to fruit. There are, though, many ornamental varieties that succeed well. Normally, the safest course is to get a young plant from someone who is already growing one, and to take any advice that may be readily given.

Philodendron scandens

Philodendron is a huge genus, many species of which can be grown in an intermediate or stove house. There are a number of good species and varieties, but *P. scandens* and *P. melanochrysum* are two of the best. One of the most popular, *P. scandens* is an excellent climber with fairly 'heavy' stems which, when they become long enough, hang down rather than climb. This leaves other stems, and shorter ones, to carry on climbing.

P. melanochrysum (previously better known as *P. Andreanum*) is a completely different plant from *P. scandens*. It is much less tall and with large, shield-shaped, velvety, dark green leaves fully 30cm (12in) long.

Philodendrons prefer partial shade to direct sunshine and this should go with a humid atmosphere – exactly the conditions that are found in a 'serious' stove house.

Scindapsus aureus

Now known as *Epipremnum aureum*, *Scindapsus aureus* is very similar to *Philodendron scandens* in that it has heart-shaped, fleshy leaves, a stout stem and a climbing habit. The difference is that it has many and various varieties. Most have bright green leaves with different forms of variegation, some of which is yellow and some white. A particularly good form is 'Marble Queen', whose leaves contain more white than green and its colours speckled almost 50/50.

6 Growing Vegetables in a Greenhouse

It is possible to grow a very useful range of vegetables in a greenhouse, although the choice is more limited than with flowers, mainly because it is neither feasible nor economical to grow many of them. For example, brassicas are out for two reasons: they would take up too much room for too long a time, and in any case they are perfectly easy to grow over a long period outdoors.

One group of vegetables to consider is those that are easy to grow outdoors but that might be wanted out of season. The only way to do that is in heat under glass. Salad vegetables such as lettuces and chicory, radishes and salad (spring) onions are all easy and popular species in this group.

In another group, there are a number of vegetables that are better when grown under heated glass, including tomatoes, aubergines, peppers, cucumbers, chicory, endive, and so on. In many locations these grow more successfully under glass than in the open, and in some of the colder and more exposed situations, the greenhouse is the only place where it is possible to grow them. Among others that can be matured during the winter where heated glass is available are mustard and cress and land cress (similar to watercress but grown on dry land).

The final selection of what to grow will depend largely on how much room there is in the greenhouse and on the gardener's need for any or all of these edible crops. As with virtually everything else that it might be desirable to grow in the greenhouse, a list of priorities will have to be drawn up and choices made. Those choices will have to be based on what is most popular, how much room is available, how much heat can be 'bought' and the amount of work that will be involved. If budget is an important consideration, try to choose those vegetables that are the most expensive to buy. It is pointless filling up the greenhouse with edibles that are cheap to buy locally. It is also unwise to be too ambitious. It is much more impressive to grow easier crops well than difficult ones badly.

TOMATOES

Tomatoes are undoubtedly one of the most popular crops for amateurs to grow. They do not need a great deal of heat, they are easy to grow, and it takes a special kind of gardener to make a mess of them. Cucumbers come close to tomatoes for popularity, but they require completely different growing conditions from tomatoes. Cucumbers like it hot and wet; tomatoes prefer it cool and moderately dry. Thus, if the two are grown together in the same greenhouse, conditions will normally suit one and not the other – or they will suit neither. At best, results will be mediocre.

One of the most common diseases of cucumbers, and other cucurbits such as courgettes and melons, is 'neck rot' around the stem at the point where it enters the compost. This is caused by keeping the compost too wet, allowing the fungus to develop. The rot progresses quite quickly and often when the first sign of it is visible, the plant is already doomed. Prevention is simple: when planting the cucumber, make sure that the top of the rootball is about an inch above the compost. In this way, the base of the stem and the top of the rootball stay dry and the fungus cannot establish itself.

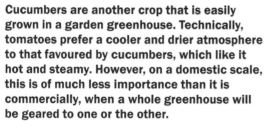

Cucumbers are another crop that is easily grown in a garden greenhouse. Technically, tomatoes prefer a cooler and drier atmosphere to that favoured by cucumbers, which like it hot and steamy. However, on a domestic scale, this is of much less importance than it is commercially, when a whole greenhouse will be geared to one or the other.

Tomatoes are more tolerant of imperfect growing conditions than cucumbers and this is the reason why they are such a good crop for beginners. By far the easiest way to grow them is in a growbag, which provides all the right conditions.

The time to sow tomatoes for greenhouse cultivation is during the first half of March. As a guide, 18–20°C (65–68°F) is a good temperature range to aim for. If it is much warmer, germination will still take place but subsequent growth will almost certainly be lanky and 'drawn' in the poor light conditions.

The seeds may be sown in cell trays, with individual cells of no more than 2cm (under an inch) across, one seed per cell. The seeds are large enough to do this quite easily; otherwise, tweezers can be used.

About a month after sowing, the seedlings will be large enough to pot up, with quite a few roots being seen through the drainage holes in the base of each cell. A 7- to 8cm (3in) pot is a suitable size for the first potting, with one seedling per pot. The seedlings should be at the 'cotyledon' stage, that is, with just the two seed leaves open.

After potting up, the seed leaves should be only just above the surface of the compost. This will lead to roots growing from the buried stem of the tiny plant so that it will make a stronger plant more quickly.

When the pot is full of roots a few weeks later, a further potting into 7- to 8-cm (3-in) pots is carried out. The compost should simply cover the rootball.

The next move, some weeks later, is the final one, straight into the cropping position; whether that is in growbags, cardboard pots or the ground. A standard growbag will accommodate three tomato plants in a greenhouse, four outdoors. An alternative to planting straight into a bag is to plant into the large 'cardboard', bottomless pots that are often called 'whalehide' pots. They are named after the firm that introduced them, with the name reflecting the strength of the man-made material from which they are constructed. For this type of planting, the bags are slit open as directed and the 'pots' are placed in position and filled with soil-less potting compost. The young tomato plants are planted into this compost. This system has the advantage that the roots have more compost to grow into and, thus, make better plants that should crop more heavily.

Whichever system is used, the plants should be loosely tied to 1-m (3-ft) canes, which are pushed into the compost close to them, as soon as they need support. When they reach the top of the canes, a wire is stretched about another 1m (3ft) above the plants, along either the ridge of the greenhouse or the inside timbers (whichever is more appropriate). Three- or five-ply fillis, from the garden centre, is fine for this as it is soft and strong. As the plant grows, it is at first looped round the fillis and, later,

loosely tied to it. When it reaches the end, the top is taken out above a leaf.

Greenhouse tomatoes are, according to their variety, grown either as a 'bush' or 'trained'. The 'bush' varieties are allowed to grow at will, need very little attention and are often planted in the ground outdoors or singly in pots in the greenhouse. The single-stem, trained varieties are the best

De-leafing tomatoes is something that is done once the plants start to crop. When the first fruits on a truss are turning orange, the leaves below that truss are best removed, because they have done their job of feeding the truss above them and are no longer required. They are using water unprofitably and are going to start dying off anyway – dying leaves are the first to attract harmful fungi, such as Botrytis and tomato leaf mould.

for a confined space as they have more of an ordered appearance and habit. The bush varieties are apt to take charge in a greenhouse, unless they are of a specifically dwarf variety. Trained varieties are best grown as a single stem and are supported on canes and wire (*see above*). They are kept as a single stem by removing all side-shoots that grow out from immediately above a leaf.

As well as different varieties, tomatoes also come in many different types and shapes, from the tiny bite-size ones to the huge knobbly Continental 'beefsteak' ones, and everything in between. All have their virtues and vices but they still fall into the general categories of 'trained' and 'bush'. As regards taste, this is really down to personal preference, experience and perhaps recommendation.

PEPPERS

Closely related to tomatoes, both botanically and culturally, are the many and varied pepper varieties. They require very much the same growing conditions as tomatoes and more or less the same cultivation. The

Sweet peppers (C) fruiting well in a grow-bag in a modest greenhouse during the summer.

main difference bertween the plants is that peppers are much less vigorous than tomatoes. Smaller and requiring less room, they are a much 'tidier' plant.

As with tomatoes, some varieties can be grown outdoors while others require a greenhouse. As with tomatoes, though, the greenhouse varieties are superior in quality and flavour.

As well as the more usual red or green colours, yellow, orange and even black varieties exist. Their shape also varies, from almost round to the scorchingly hot little ones which are shaped like a small, bright red French bean. Their flavours and heat, in culinary terms, also vary. The hot pepper varieties are not to everyone's liking but the large-fruited ones have the typical and very pleasant taste.

Some people have a violent allergic reaction to peppers, so be warned if you have not eaten them before.

A fine home-grown sweet pepper (C). These and the hot little chilli peppers (C) are very easy to grow at home and make a colourful addition to a greenhouse.

AUBERGINE

The other greenhouse vegetable that has gained popularity over the years is the eggplant, or aubergine. This needs similar growing conditions to the pepper and tomato but is the least tolerant of the cold. In fact, despite there being varieties that can just about be grown outdoors in a sheltered and sunny spot, these are poor substitutes for the 'real thing' – those grown in a greenhouse. If there is access to a greenhouse, it is not worth considering growing them outdoors. Even those varieties intended for outdoor cultivation are poor in comparison.

OTHER VEGETABLES

Tomatoes, cucumbers, peppers and aubergines are the most popular and most successful vegetables that can be grown in a greenhouse, whether heated or not, but there are other vegetables that can be forced (to maturity) under glass. These include new potatoes grown in boxes; beetroot; parsley and other herbs; French beans; pinched runner beans; courgettes; spring onions; radishes; rhubarb, seakale and chicory for blanching in the dark; and baby parsnips, carrots and turnips.

Chicory (C) is an easily grown vegetable and a boon to the winter kitchen. The best system is to grow some in the garden and, once the leaves have died down in early winter, lift them, and trim off what is left of the leaves along with the smaller side roots. What remains will look something like a cleaned-up parsnip and these can then be stored outdoors in sand or cinders. If a few of these cleaned-up roots are potted up every month or so during the winter, and kept dark and under the greenhouse staging, they will produce a supply of blanched lettuce-like leaves for winter salads.

7 Growing Fruit Under Glass

Fruit may not be the first crop that comes to mind when considering what to grow in a greenhouse, yet, just as it is easy to use a greenhouse for the cultivation of some unusual vegetables, so it is with fruit. The most appropriate fruits can be divided into two main groups: first, those fruits that it is not possible to grow outdoors because it is not warm enough; and second, those fruits that grow perfectly well outdoors but might be required to ripen earlier.

The first group includes those that naturally come from the Mediterranean area, or other parts of the world with a similar climate.

Several of these can be grown successfully in a greenhouse, where they will produce fruit of a much higher standard than when grown outdoors. Grapes are the obvious example. Figs are another example – some varieties are hardy enough to produce a worthwhile crop outside whereas others are not. Kiwi fruit are a borderline case. Some years ago, a number of commercial tomato growers in the Channel Isles stopped growing tomatoes and other salad crops and grew kiwi fruit instead. This is not suggesting that gardeners should do the same but it illustrates the point that different crops may require the same sort of growing conditions.

Peaches (C) are a natural for a cool greenhouse. They will grow perfectly well outside in a good summer but there is no chance of that happening every year so a greenhouse is the answer. As a compromise, small, untrained trees can be grown in pots, which can be stood outside whenever the weather makes it possible. To prevent the fungus disease peach leaf curl, the foliage must be kept dry; the easiest way of achieving this is in a greenhouse.

An old vinery house now given over to figs. The fig (C or outside) is a Mediterranean plant and very few varieties will ripen a crop outdoors in cooler areas. The exception is 'Brown Turkey'. Even this, though, will have the shoot ends killed in a severe winter and with them the following summer's crop. 'White Marsailles' and 'White Ischia' are two good greenhouse varieties.

The second large group consists of hardy fruits whose plants happen to be of a convenient size for growing in a greenhouse, where they will produce an earlier and possibly a higher-quality crop than they would if grown in the open. For the average gardener who cannot be bothered with 'complicated' crops such as figs and grapes, strawberries are the obvious choice. They will ripen a month or so ahead of outdoor crops and the same may be the case with raspberries, although they can be problematic. Peaches and apricots can also be included, especially in colder districts.

Even a greenhouse without heat will accelerate ripening, and a heated one will give even more flexibility. However, growing fruit in a greenhouse simply to produce an earlier crop than is possible outdoors is not always worthwhile. This is because, in a 'general-purpose' greenhouse, the plants would have to be movable. This means that the crop would have to be grown in some sort of container, so that it could be moved out of the greenhouse after fruiting. This can only be sensibly done with a naturally small plant, which limits the choice to bush fruits (currants, and so on), cane fruits and strawberries. Small fruit trees growing in pots would be a complete waste of greenhouse space, other than when they are in blossom and can be moved in overnight if a frost threatens. Normally, the yield would be too small to warrant the space that they occupied. Raspberries would have to be in large pots, their height would make them a nuisance, and only thornless varieties would be practical.

STRAWBERRIES

Strawberries are ideal for early cropping in a greenhouse and more or less any of today's varieties are perfectly satisfactory. The story begins in late summer, when new strawberry plants are either propagated at home or bought in.

The first decision to be made is the sort of container they are going to be grown in and how many of them will be needed (both plants and containers). The weight is an important consideration – they will be out of doors until the late winter, when they will have to be moved into the greenhouse. The traditional container is a terracotta strawberry barrel, which has 'pockets' around it for the plants to be grown in. The main drawback is its weight, especially when it is full of damp potting compost (which should always be soil-less for this reason) and plants. There are, however, several different designs and sizes to choose from and one of the best is the 'Towerpot'. Made of good, strong plastic, it is very light when empty. It is made in three tiers which, during the winter, can be put singly on the ground, with three plants in each.

The simplest and probably the cheapest container of all is a growbag. There should be room in a standard-sized bag for ten strawberry plants.

In late summer, the container(s) should be planted with young strawberry plants raised from the current year's rooted runners, and then kept outdoors throughout the autumn and winter. This means that the young plants are subjected to the snow and ice that they must have before they will produce fruit.

In late winter (late February in the northern hemisphere) the plants are moved into the greenhouse; obviously, this job will be easier with lighter containers. If the Towerpot is being used, this is the time to put the three tiers together, after moving them individually. The pots are kept in good light but with very little heat. If it is too warm, the plants will put too much into growing rather than fruiting. The plants will flower first and then produce fruit, normally in late spring.

This is an excellent way of advancing the strawberry season and, with the outdoor crop following shortly after the greenhouse ones, strawberries can be picked for a month or more. (If cold stored runners are planted outdoors to fruit after the normal outdoor crop, the season can be extended still further.)

It is not worth trying to save money by keeping the potted plants for a second year, as they will always fail. After strawberry plants have fruited just once in a container of any kind, they should be thrown out. This is not being wasteful; it is simply good practice. The only use to which the plants can be put is as 'mother' plants, not fruiting plants. Tip them out of the container, plant them in a spare corner of garden and, when they produce runners, root these for fruiting in the following year.

FIGS

Figs will benefit particularly from spending part of their annual life in a greenhouse. They are not at all difficult to grow, although many beginners expect them to be. If possible, the tree should be a one- or two-year-old and it is potted into, preferaby, a clay pot some 25cm (10in) across. If its root system is very small, then a smaller pot can probably be used. In any event, the tree is likely to need another two years before it fruits.

Once the roots begin to feel cramped in the pot, growth will slow down and fruiting

will start. The art is to maintain the balance between growing and fruiting. Too much of either will result in too little of the other.

Pruning an established fig in a pot is very simple. The aim is to keep the tree neat and tidy. The pot will stop the tree getting too big. If it is a young tree that has not been pruned at all, it is likely to have just a few shoots 30cm (12in) or so in length. There may be just one shoot, but that does not matter. To form a compact tree, the shoot(s) is (are) cut back by about half its (their) length after planting or, if a container-grown tree was bought, in its first winter. That is all that needs doing for the moment.

Early in the following summer, nip back the tips of all new shoots (those that have just grown) to four or five leaves. This will encourage more side shoots to form. By the end of the summer, most of the new shoots will, hopefully, have embryo 'figlets' in the leaf axils at the tips. It is not a worry if they do not; they will at some stage. Only two or three of the smallest (smaller than pea size) on each shoot should be retained, and the larger ones should be nipped off. If the tree is kept outdoors (as it should be), the larger figlets will be killed off during the winter anyway. Only the tiny ones nearest the tip will survive and it is these that will grow into figs the following summer.

Although this refers particularly to figs growing outdoors, especially those trained against a sunny wall, all fig trees will benefit from the removal of these larger figlets before the winter. Although they are green, they will be killed. They are nothing more than a burden to the tree and a hindrance to the smaller ones that are going to survive, grow and ripen next summer. Just two or three figlets should be left on each shoot tip to go through the winter and ripen in the following summer.

GRAPES

The other group of fruits that give their best performance when grown in a greenhouse comprise the really choice varieties of grape; such as Muscat of Alexandria (white) and Black Hamburgh. These are planted in the ground, either inside or outside the greenhouse. If planted outside, the vine should be close to the wall of the greenhouse and then led inside through a brick-sized hole made at ground level. It is restricted to just one shoot and this is trained up the inside of the roof glass, and 'stopped' (nipping out the growing point) when it reaches the ridge.

The single shoot is the only permanent part of the vine and it is from this that the horizontal fruiting shoots grow out each year. These fruiting shoots are trained horizontally and sideways from each side of the vertical shoot. They are allowed to grow until embryo flower buds are seen on them. They are then stopped when two leaves have formed beyond the flower cluster. It is these flower clusters that will develop into bunches of grapes. From that point on, all new shoots that appear from anywhere on the vine are stopped at two leaves.

The fruit will be picked at the end of the summer or in the early autumn, depending on the variety.

Once the vine has gone completely dormant in the early winter, the horizontal shoots that carried the grapes are cut hard back to the main vertical cane and the whole sequence starts all over again in the spring.

In a small greenhouse, it is best to restrict the size of the vine. If it is allowed to grow bigger, it could take up the whole of one side of the roof glass, allowing very little light in for other plants. In this case, it might be better to use a system of cultivation whereby the grape plant is grown in a pot. For a number of reasons, it is usual to grow these potted plants on a 'leg' (stem) about 1.25m (4ft) tall. Like any other plant, the vine is moved into a larger pot when necessary. Strictly speaking, it should not be allowed to carry fruit until it is in its final (largest) pot but it takes great determination not to allow any grapes to form during the build-up period. Taking one bunch a year once the vine is a couple of years old will not hurt the plant, but it will slow its growth.

For a beginner, simply because they are easier to manage, American varieties are good ones to start with. Of these, 'Fragola' is very rewarding. Its name derives from Fragaria, the botanical name for the strawberry, and it and the 'Strawberry grape', which is probably the same, both carry small, pink fruits.

Temperature-wise, grapes are easily pleased and the majority are quite happy with the conditions found in a 'general' greenhouse. However, some of the really choice varieties do need a more specialized environment.

To see grapes grown to perfection, visit the Royal Horticultural Society's October Show in London.

CITRUS

Like grapes, the Citrus family is largely of Mediterranean origin and, as such, does not require anything too unusual by way of growing conditions. It is a very large genus with some most peculiar-looking species and hybrids, but it is really the oranges, lemons, grapefruits and limes that interest the general gardener, with perhaps one or two peculiarities catching the eye. One of the strangest of these peculiar varieties is *Citrus medica* 'Etrog', the 'Fingered citron' or 'Buddha's hand'. The fruit is about the size of a normal lemon but is split into finger-like segments, each of which is covered with normal citrus 'peel'. The species dates back to about 4000BC and this particular variety appears to have no reason for existing other than as a curiosity.

Virtually all Citrus can be grown in an average, general-purpose cool greenhouse with a minimum temperature of around 7°C (44°F). They can be grown very successfully in JIP3, and must be well firmed in or they produce a lot of spindly growth and correspondingly poor flowers and fruit. Although they need to be well watered throughout the growing season, they need drier conditions during dormancy and, naturally for a Mediterranean plant, really sharp drainage.

Red spider mite and scale insect can be a nuisance if not controlled.

Most commercial Citrus plants are propagated by grafting on to other Citrus seedlings but summer cuttings about 10cm (4in) long are equally successful.

8   Pest and Disease Control

Inevitably, there has to be a downside to greenhouse gardening and undoubtedly its least friendly face is represented by pests and diseases. Fortunately, weeds play little part in greenhouse gardening at this level but, sadly, pests and diseases do have a more significant role in greenhouse gardening than in outdoor gardening. This is perfectly logical really. A greenhouse provides conditions for growth that are not available outdoors, enabling the gardener to grow a wider range of plants than is possible in the open garden. In addition, a greenhouse can be used to grow familiar plants, but encouraging them to mature at a different time from the usual.

Growing either category of plant involves warmer conditions than those that prevail outside. That is the whole point of having a greenhouse. However, providing warmth and, less often, daylight at a time when it would normally be a good deal cooler and darker, also provides a mcro-climate that will encourage the arrival and survival of organisms that are neither wanted nor expected. These undesirables come together under the general heading of 'pests and diseases'.

Broadly speaking, pests and diseases are living organisms that prey upon the plants being cultivated, in this case under glass. In simple terms, a pest is normally a creature with legs and/or wings, together with a head, thorax and abdomen. It causes damage to a plant usually, but not always, by eating it or sucking the sap from it. In either case, the plant is usually ruined. In most cases, it can move about. A disease, on the other hand, can certainly spread from one place to another but it cannot move about in the same way.

Besides these two examples there is a whole world of other organisms, frequently microscopic, that do not fall easily into either category. These are the viruses and bacteria that can attack plants with equally disastrous results.

Unfortunately, all these organisms have it within their power to ruin, and often kill, a gardener's plants in order to stay alive themselves. The first 'law' of pest and disease control is to act quickly when trouble is first seen. If pests or diseases are either not seen or are ignored when they are seen, it is a recipe for disaster. Doing nothing in the hope that they will disappear is fatal – they will not.

PREVENTIVE MEASURES

The physical control of individual pests, diseases and other parasites comes later and, in many cases, it involves the use of a chemical. Before that – and this is something that many gardeners fail to appreciate – there are a number of measures that can, and should, be taken to discourage and/or prevent pests and diseases from becoming established:

- be observant and act quickly, should the need arise;

- make an effort to provide conditions that will encourage healthy and strong plants – a strong plant is much less likely to be damaged by a pest or disease than a weak and feeble one. By the same token, a strong plant will be better able to withstand an attack;
- avoid creating conditions that are likely to encourage pests and diseases;
- attend to ventilation, to discourage stagnant air within the greenhouse so that fungal diseases are less likely to appear and/or spread;
- at the same time, ventilation is also the obvious way to avoid overheating within the greenhouse. Overheating is clearly detrimental to plants;
- try to keep plants at an even temperature in a greenhouse. A wide range of plants will inevitably mean that some plants will enjoy the conditions whereas others may not;
- eliminate alternative hosts. Many pests and diseases will live quite happily on more than one kind of host plant. If the alternative hosts are weeds, clearly they are playing an important part in the survival and spread of that pest or disease;
- 'crop rotation' in the outdoor vegetable garden is an important factor in preventing the spread or build-up of particular pests and diseases. The situation is the same, although to a lesser extent, in a greenhouse;
- the management of greenhouse gardening involves the use of resistant varieties. Plant breeders are doing all that they can to breed new varieties of flowers and vegetables that are less likely to fall victim to specific pests and diseases. These should be grown whenever they are available and suitable.

NON-CHEMICAL CONTROL

In terms of management, therefore, there is much that can be done to reduce the incidence of pests and diseases in the greenhouse. However, some will still find their way in. What can be done next, before chemicals need to be brought into the picture? It has to be said that the use of non-chemical control systems, sometimes referred to as the 'organic' approach, is likely to be less effective than using chemicals. However, it can give a good measure of control where, for one reason or another, the use of chemicals is undesirable. In addition, it cannot discriminate between harmful and harmless creatures, and a number of beneficial insects that prey on the pests will be destroyed too.

There are a number of 'non-chemical' methods of control. In the open garden, the range of gadgets and contrivances goes back to what is probably the oldest deterrent of all: the scarecrow. At least in the short term, it does an excellent job of keeping birds away from crops. Without a scarecrow, a crop of brassicas, such as winter cabbages, Brussels sprouts and next year's spring cabbages, can be decimated by pigeons during a hard winter. Netting can also be very effective when thrown over crops to be protected.

Neither of these would apply in the greenhouse, of course, but there are several similar methods that will help the greenhouse gardener. If slugs are a nuisance among over-wintering greenhouse lettuces, there are a number of devices and traps that are very effective at either deterring or actually destroying them. In addition, the traditional slug pellets may be acceptable. Although chemical-based, they are less damaging than, say, chemical sprays. They are distributed exactly where they are wanted and the molluscicides that they contain are specifically poisonous only to slugs and snails.

Sticky yellow traps, based on the fly-paper principle, are excellent against white-fly in a greenhouse. In fact, they combine two methods of control: yellow attracts a whole host of insects, both damaging and harmless, and, of course, the sticky feature will trap anything that has been attracted by the yellow and lands on it. Single traps of this kind should last a whole growing season.

Working on the same principle, special grease is available for smearing on the edge of greenhouse staging, or around the rim of pots to trap adult vine weevils. This is a particularly unpleasant pest with the adults staying hidden in the day. They are normally active only at night, when they venture out and lay their eggs in the compost in which pot plants are growing. Cyclamen are a favourite host, as are fuchsias. The eggs hatch to produce maggots that feed on the roots of the host plant and cause it to collapse and, often, die. When the grease is used, the adults are trapped on it and can be squashed. The weevil's shell is surprisingly hard so it is usually best to pick it off, put it on paving or a brick floor and tread on it.

'Companion planting' is another non-chemical system of pest control that sometimes proves effective. It involves growing certain plants among the crop plants and works on the basis of the companion plants' smell being unpleasant to specific pests, and therefore keeping them away from the plants that need to be protected. Alternatively, the scent of the companion plant may be so strong as to 'hide' the smell of the crop from the pests, which then go off in search of food elsewhere. The method gives a degree of control but it can be difficult for the grower to judge just how much.

As regards the non-chemical control of fungal disease in the greenhouse, there really is nothing that is reliably effective. The most important weapon against fungal disease, such as grey mould (Botrytis) on tomatoes, is good management – that is, avoiding conditions that are conducive to the spread of disease. The vast majority of plant diseases are fungal and most fungi are encouraged by ad lib watering and a complete lack of understanding about a plant's needs for water.

Virus diseases, in most cases, are passed from plant to plant by insects, so vigilant pest control is vital. Another way of preventing virus diseases is by making sure that all plants that are brought into the greenhouse come from a reputable source. Be wary of accepting plant gifts of uncertain origin and be aware that even plants of known origin cannot be guaranteed to be free from infection.

BIOLOGICAL CONTROL

One system of pest and disease elimination that has been seen to be particularly effective in recent years, both on a commercial and garden scale, is biological control. This involves the introduction to the greenhouse of natural enemies of, usually, specific pests and diseases. It is also known as 'natural control', as it reflects what goes on in the wild, and it does not involve chemicals.

The method involves looking for an 'agent' that preys upon a particular pest, for example, glasshouse whitefly. Several companies sell these agents to private gardeners, as well as to commercial growers, and they all advertise in the gardening press at appropriate times of the year.

The two most significant pests in the world of the amateur greenhouse gardener are whitefly and red spider mite, which can both cause extensive damage. There are non-chemical controls for whitefly, such as yellow sticky traps, but there is a limit to how effective they can be. In the same way, red spider mite can be 'discouraged', but not killed, by keeping the atmosphere in the greenhouse humid, but this may cause other problems – a damp atmosphere during cool weather can lead to Botrytis and other fungal diseases.

The answer may lie in biological control, which involves the purchase and release into the greenhouse of certain creatures. As long as it is warm enough, these will feed on both whitefly and red spider mite, and keep them down to a more or less harmless level. The whitefly predator is *Encarsia formosa* and that of the red spider mite is another mite, *Phytoseiulus persimilis*. Both are widely available, either direct from the producers or at many garden centres. It is important to follow closely the instructions provided with the predators. They are living things and, as such, are subject to their own limitations.

The list of available parasites and predators is increasing the whole time and, before long, home gardeners are likely to have available a formidable army with which to tackle the greenhouse pest problem.

CHEMICAL CONTROL

In spite of all the alternative methods, there is still a long way to go before chemical control, of one sort or another, can be forgotten. Everything possible should be done to encourage predators, parasites and other beneficial agents to thrive in the greenhouse, but at some point chemical remedies may have to be called upon. They should only be used, however, when other methods have proved ineffective or inadequate, and of course if the gardener has no ethical objection to them.

In the ever-changing world of chemical control – changing in terms of what can legally be used and what is available from shops and garden centres – it is impossible to give any firm and specific recommendations as to what should be used to control a specific pest or disease. There are, however, several broad pieces of advice that will always apply:

1 Correct identification of the pest or disease is vital if the correct remedy is to be found. This applies either to the pathogen (pest or disease) itself and/or to the symptoms of attack (the damge that has been done). If it is not possible to identify the culprit with any degree of certainty, a sample should be taken to the local garden centre for an expert opinion. Hopefully, they will be able to help with identification and with supplying a remedy.

2 Be wary of 'helpful' but amateur advice, unless it comes from a reliable source. If it is incorrect, it will not only be useless but could also be expensive, in terms of buying the wrong remedy and in having to replace a dead plant.

3 Having identified the problem, especially whether it is a pest or disease, decide on the best chemical control and on the best formulation to use (*see below*).

4 Last, it is vital to follow the general guidelines when applying the chemicals and to read carefully any specific instructions given with the chosen product.

All that has been said about chemicals for pest and disease control in the greenhouse applies equally to their use outdoors.

Formulation

The choice of spray will be narrowed down by determining whether the pest is a sucking one, such as an aphid (greenfly), or a biting and chewing one such as a caterpillar. For the sucking pest, a 'systemic' material is to be preferred because the pest feeds on sap and a systemic material enters that plant and its sap stream. For a caterpillar, a 'contact' material is marginally more effective. The caterpillar eats mouthfuls of the plant, so covering the leaf surface with insecticide is likely to give the best control.

Another approach is to use an insecticide that will land on the culprit, enter it through its skin and kill it that way. These materials will normally also kill the pest as a stomach poison.

Vine weevil larvae may be controlled by drenching the compost in the pots with a suitable insecticide. This is best done applying enough of the diluted material so that a small amount runs out of the drainage holes in the bottom of the pot. Aerosols are normally based on the same insecticides but come in aerosol form. These are probably more useful in a smaller greenhouse, where mixing a gallon or so of the material will give far more than is needed.

Some insecticides are also available as dusts. These are more often used when treating, for example, ants' nests and other sites, as opposed to plants. They have no particular benefit over sprays and aerosols, except that it is easier to see exactly where they have been applied. Dusts can be unsightly when applied to flowers.

Fungicides (pesticides that kill harmful fungi) are also available as contact and systemic formulations and follow the same general rules.

General Guidelines for Application

- Wear protective clothing when necessary. The minimum is a pair of rubber gloves.
- Avoid breathing in dry formulations, such as pesticidal dusts.
- Spray drift can be dangerous in windy weather; do not work in it.
- When applying more than one chemical in a single spray, add the concentrates one at a time to the water. Do not mix the concentrates.
- Unless it is specifically advised against, foliar feeds can be added to sprays; this is a useful way of feeding the plants at the same time.
- Do not spray during sunshine as it can cause scorch.
- Do not apply sprays or dusts when there are beneficial insects on the plants.
- Always treat thoroughly. Failure to do so can lead to a poor kill of pests and may cause resistance to build up among them.
- Always dispose of empty containers and unused diluted chemicals safely.
- Contact your local authority about the disposal of unwanted concentrates.

Index

RELATED TITLES
FROM CROWOOD

Container Gardening

KATHY BROWN

ISBN 978 1 84797 275 0
144pp, 292 illustrations

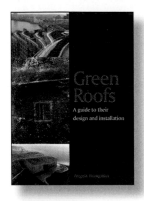

Green Roofs
A guide to their design and installation

ANGELA YOUNGMAN

ISBN 978 1 84797 296 5
144pp, 134 illustrations

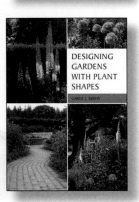

Designing Gardens With Plant Shapes

CAROL J. SMITH

ISBN 978 1 84797 279 8
128pp, 178 illustrations

Planting Design Essentials

JILL ANDERSON & PAMELA JOHNSON

ISBN 978 1 84797 270 5
160pp, 158 illustrations

Designing Small Gardens

IAN COOKE

ISBN 978 1 84797 290 3
144pp, 116 illustrations

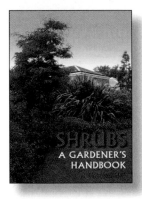

Shrubs
A gardener's handbook

IAN COOKE

ISBN 978 1 84797 312 2
144pp, 151 illustrations

In case of difficulty ordering, contact the Sales Office:

The Crowood Press Ltd
Ramsbury
Wiltshire
SN8 2HR
UK

Tel: 44 (0) 1672 520320
enquiries@crowood.com
www.crowood.com